FROM LORD TO FATHER

CHANGING THE NATURE OF OUR RELATIONSHIP WITH GOD

RALPH HALE

Author of Taking Dictation and Christ at the Center

ISBN 979-8-89588-626-7

For Vicki
Our relationship with one another grows stronger
as our relationship with the Father grows deeper.

Contents

The Transition

01

My father and I had a rather complicated relationship.

The world that he grew up in was as foreign to my privileged middleclass childhood as any two cultures could possibly be. The son of a sharecropper in rural Arkansas, he experienced the Great Depression from the perspective of an endless cotton field (owned by someone else) that had to be picked every season for a small share of the crop. He was one of those skinny kids (head down; with grown-up eyes) that you see in the old black and white photographs from the dust bowl days. My father didn't talk much about his childhood, but you could see the evidence of it in the lines of his face and the premature gray in his hair. World War II provided a way of escape from the cotton field, and after serving in the Army Air Corp, he took advantage of the G.I. bill and became the first in his family to receive a higher education. I respected him and wanted desperately to please him – but I found it difficult to really know him as my father. Throughout most of my childhood, his role in our family was that of "The Enforcer." After breaking the rules (again) I would be instructed by my longsuffering mother to, "go to your room and wait for your father to get home." When he got home, his job was to dole out the punishment that I so richly deserved. He was "old school" in his understanding of how to bring up children and would regularly administer the same kind of spankings (with a strap) that he had received as a child. I knew that he loved me, but I didn't know how to draw close to that love. The solution in our relationship was for me to simply obey orders. As I moved from high school to my college years, I allowed my father to have complete control over the planning of my future – and he decided that it would be a career in dentistry! He introduced me to several successful dentists in our town and soon I was enrolled in the pre-med program at the University of Alabama. It didn't last long. I changed majors after that first year and changed lifestyles after the second – plunging headlong into the counterculture "hippie" movement of the early seventies. Although this isn't a book about my childhood, it is about overcoming the experiences in our lives that can limit and even distort our understanding of God as Father. He also inhabits a kingdom that's very different from the world we live in. He can seem like a frightening enforcer at times – and sometimes it's just easier to say, "yes Lord" and move no closer in our relationship with him.

After many years of serving as a pastor in several different countries, I've noticed that most people who come to Christ have a tendency to usually divide into two very distinct groups. One quickly grows from babyhood to maturity as they discover God's plans and purposes for their lives. Fruit seems to come easily and in a short time they are serving and blessing others. The second group, however, seems to reach a kind of plateau in their Christian growth. They are regular church attenders, but their lives are perhaps a little too regular. Something is missing. I eventually became convinced that what is missing is not a knowledge of the Bible or a person's giftings or religious convictions – but the *type of relationship* they have with God. We understand that there is more than one type of relationship that we can have with another person. The way that we relate to our boss is very different from the way that we relate to our co-workers. Our relationship with our spouse differs from the way we might relate to other family members. Most people also instinctively understand that there are transitions in those relationships. Our association with a co-worker can have several stages, ranging from acquaintance to friend to confidant. A girlfriend (or boyfriend) can transition from lover to partner to that mysterious relationship the Bible calls "One Flesh." However, when it comes to our relationship with God, we don't seem to realize that there are also transitions. Many Christians have pretty much the same kind of relationship that they started with after coming to God: one of Savior and Lord. Their level of intimacy with him has seen little change since those early days. This condition can have many explanations, but perhaps the most common one is this – many believers don't see that God also is a "being." He is not a created being as we are, but he is most surely a unique and personal being who has chosen to create human beings in his own image. One of the most radical aspects of the Bible is that it presents God in this way: not as an unknowable force, but as a living and feeling personality! Throughout scripture we are introduced to a God who speaks and loves and knows us in the most intimate of ways; and this points to the first important concept that we must understand if we are going to make the transition from Lord to Father...

We were always meant to know him

The Bible not only describes God as a personal being, it also presents him as one who can be experienced in the same way that we experience others in our lives. In the great prayer of Jesus recorded in John chapter 17, it's easy to overlook a crucial principle of our Christianity that's right at the beginning of that prayer. "Now this is eternal life: that they know you, the only true God" (John 17:3). According to Jesus, what constitutes life that is real and eternal? "That they may know you." The knowledge of God was never meant to be some kind of rigid theology or ambiguous feeling. David invited us to, "Taste and see that the Lord is good" (Psalm 34:8). Jesus said, "The sheep listen to his voice. He calls his own sheep by name and leads them out" (John 10:3). The promise to those who would yield their lives to God was always that we could have much more than just a deeper religious experience. In Matthew 5:8 it says, "Blessed are the pure in heart, for they will *see* God." However, this transition from Lord to Father can never happen unless we fully realize that – God wants it to happen! He desires more than loyal servants doing his will, he wants loving children who are learning to know him better. So, if we were always meant to know him in an intimate way as Father, what keeps this transition from happening? The answer to that question can be summed up in a little-known principle that has a well-known effect on every Christian's life...

What we experience in the physical determines how we perceive the spiritual.

One of the great misconceptions that people have about the physical and spiritual world is that they are in totally separate spheres that are unconnected and unaffected by one another. Most of us understand that we can't live one life in the physical and a different life in the spiritual, but we don't always appreciate how our experience in one greatly affects our perception of the other! This is true on many different levels: Our experience in an overly conservative church can negatively color our view of Christianity. Disappointments in life can create a mistrust in the basic goodness of God. However, nowhere is this principle more aptly demonstrated than in our experiences growing up with our earthly father.

"FATHER." Most people find it hard to even pronounce that name in a neutral way. With all of us, it is a name that is filled with memories and experiences that are both beautiful and painful. There are many fortunate people who grew up with good fathers; men who loved them and generously gave of their time and attention. For those blessed people, it's not very difficult to realize, "Hey, God is like my Dad." But for many others, childhood was a very different kind of experience. Learning how to manage an angry father who was violent and unpredictable. Settling for a distant father who was cold and unapproachable. Growing up without the influence of a father in their lives. For those people, there is an urgent, persistent inner voice warning, "Be careful, you know how fathers are!" Bible study and church attendance have very little effect on this distorted picture of "father" that is painted upon their hearts. So how does one change this false inner portrait that many of us have of Father? Scripture gives an intriguing answer. "For the Spirit that God has given you does not make you slaves and cause you to be afraid; instead, the Spirit makes you God's children, and by the Spirit's power we cry out to God, 'Father! my Father'" (Roman 8:15 GNB). If it is true that only by the Spirit's power we cry out "Father my Father" then we must understand that the entire process, from first to last, is solely a work of the Holy Spirit! Most of us are familiar (at least theoretically) with the work of the Holy Spirit. We believe in his power to heal as well as his ability to convict the world of sin, of righteousness and of the judgment to come (See John 16:8). However, we don't really grasp that, apparently, it is only by the Spirit's power that we can say "Father!" How exactly does the Holy Spirit change our perception of Father?

Repainting the picture

There is a little-known fact in the world of classical art that gives a good illustration of how this process works. Over the years, the curators of some of the world's biggest museums have discovered an interesting secret: if you take an x-ray of some of the great masterpieces, you discover that there is, sometimes, another painting hidden underneath! Behind Vincent van Gough's 1885 work entitled "Head of a Peasant Woman" there is a self-portrait of the artist himself. In Rembrandt's masterpiece, "Old Man in Military Costume" modern x-ray techniques discovered the image of a hidden "Younger Man in a Military Costume." Why did they do it? The most obvious reason is that they weren't happy with the quality of the original. Because so many started off as penniless artists, it was more economical to paint over the inferior picture rather than buy a new canvas. This illustrates a function of the Holy Spirit that we often don't consider: God has no intention to remove the experiences of our past (they are what has molded us into who we are) but he does desire to repaint the distorted image that we have of father. He understands that what we experience in the physical determines how we perceive the spiritual. Titus 3:5-6 seems to be pointing to this phenomenon when it says, "He saved us, not on the basis of deeds which we have done in righteousness, but according to His mercy, by the washing of regeneration and renewing by the Holy Spirit." Apparently, when we come to Christ, there are many things in our lives that are not only forgiven but renewed. The Holy Spirit, like the master artists of old, paints over that original portrait and begins to fashion a new image of Father in our hearts. Only the Holy Spirit is qualified to do this. In 1 Corinthians 2:10-11 it says, "The Spirit searches all things, even the deep things of God... no one knows the thoughts of God except the Spirit of God." This remarkable statement shows us that the Holy Spirit knows the Father far better than anyone else, and part of his mission in our lives is to show us those deep things that only he knows. How does he show us? I am convinced that it is primarily through His Holy Scripture. Words that have been preserved and protected and placed into the hands of people. One purpose of this book is to allow God's Holy Spirit to work in exactly this way: to be the paintbrush that dips into his word and paints a vibrant and accurate portrait of the Father. It's not enough to just begin our prayers with "Our Father who art in heaven" we must allow him to reveal our Father in heaven who has chosen to live in our hearts!

Questions to Consider

1.   Take a moment and try to look honestly at the *type* of relationship that you have with God. Is it a Lord-relationship (where you mostly look for orders coming from an authority figure) or is it a Father-relationship (marked by love and intimacy)?

2.   Why do you think that a Lord-relationship is insufficient in order to grow to maturity as a Christ-follower?

3.   What kind of portrait of father was painted in your heart as you transitioned from childhood to your adult years? Say the word, "FATHER" out loud; what image appears in your mind?

4.   Can you make a list of five or more things that honestly describe your earthly father's character and personality? How do these characteristics color your image of your heavenly Father?

5.   If knowing God as Father is primarily a work of the Holy Spirit, how does this change your understanding in how you are to transition in your relationship from Lord to Father?

His Love

CHAPTER
02

"If you had the power to create your own perfect earthly father – what would he be like?' That's a question I would frequently ask young missionaries-in-training in Youth With A Mission back in the 1980s. I was living in one of the inner-city slums of Manila in the Philippines, and our team had planted a church for the poor that worked alongside a small health clinic. I was only recently trained myself, but soon I was teaching about the Father-Heart of God in YWAM Discipleship Training Schools throughout Southeast Asia. The students came from widely different cultures and backgrounds, but over time, I started to see a pattern in the way they described a perfect father. There was always one characteristic at the top of the list; a feature of a good father that seemed to occur to everyone right away. But there was also another characteristic that was almost always at the bottom of the list; and it sometimes did not make the list at all. Yet both are essential in knowing God as father.

In this chapter, we will start with what is almost always at the top of most people's list when describing a perfect father – his love. Everyone agrees that love is an essential element of fathering, but there are many who struggle when it comes to God's love. One of the difficulties that we have in really understanding his love is that in the world, love has a very different meaning. If you ask the average person on the street, "What is love?" you would probably get one of three general kinds of answers. Some would say, "Love is a feeling." In describing that kind of love, people would talk about the feelings of attraction or the "butterfly effect" that occurs in your gut when you first lay eyes on that very special person. Love is the name of a particular emotion (or strong desire) that we feel towards another. Others might answer the question by saying, "love is a basic need." After all, the Beatles sang, "All you need is love" so love must be essential to having a good life. People who believe this will do almost anything to satisfy their need to be loved; even to the point of compromising their morals or opening their lives to questionable people. Still others might answer by saying, "love is a response." To be loved, whether by parents or a special other, you must elicit that response from them by meeting certain expectations. Many have grown up in an environment where love was given or withheld according to their grades in school or their choices in life. They sincerely believe that love must be earned, so they devote much of their lives towards trying to generate that response from others. The problem with all three of these answers is that – God's love is different! It's not a feeling that he occasionally has, or a need that must be met, or even a reward that he gives to those who have been good. His love is very different from all of those things! In this chapter, we will take three scriptures in the Bible that describe the Father's love and try to get a clearer picture of how different his love really is. Let's look at the first one.

"Dear friends, let us love one another, for love comes from God. Everyone who loves has been born of God and knows God. Whoever does not love does not know God, because God is love" (I John 4:7-8). This verse has always fascinated me. It doesn't say, "love one another, for it is your duty to love." Instead, we are told to love others for the simple reason that love comes from God. In fact, our ability to love correctly is the ultimate proof that we know (or don't know) God! Then, the Apostle John makes a truly radical statement in the next part of this verse, "For God is love." When we read that statement through the distorted lens of the world, it's easy to hear, "God feels love" or "God rewards with love." However, in these words we discover an amazing truth about God – love is something that he is! Although he is invisible and uncreated and far beyond our limited understanding, God is not a theory. He exists! The Bible doesn't say a lot about what God is, but there are clues. In John 4:24 it says, "God is spirit, and his worshipers must worship in spirit and in truth" so we get the hint that he is a spiritual being who wants to be worshiped in the spirit. But probably the most intriguing clue is here in our text which declares, "God is love." The Amplified Bible gives a good understanding of what is actually being said in the original language. "For God is love. [He is the originator of love, and it is an enduring attribute of His nature.]" (I John 4:8 The Amplified Bible). In other words, when you trace love all the way back past every possible expression of love until you reach its origin – you find the Father! This eternal fact points to what is perhaps the most important (and challenging) aspect of understanding God as Father.

His Love is Unconditional

In our text, John continues to define this aspect of Father-love when he says, "This is love: not that we loved God, but that he loved us and sent his Son as an atoning sacrifice for our sins" (I John 4:10). In other words, this is what Father-love looks like; not a response to our love, but a love that existed long before we loved him! Paul later points to this same idea in Romans 5:8 when he says, "God demonstrates his own love for us in this: While we were still sinners, Christ died for us." When you give a demonstration of something (like a vacuum cleaner salesman) you are attempting to show how it works and what its properties are like. Back in the day, it was common to find a smiling man at your front door with a vacuum cleaner in his hand. He would ask if he could give you a short demonstration, and then, after putting a little dirt on your kitchen floor, he would display the power of his vacuum by cleaning it up. The age-old idea in sales is that you must see something demonstrated before you will realize that you need it. It's interesting that when God decided to demonstrate Father-love, he chose a very similar strategy. He demonstrated unconditional love by allowing Christ to die for us long before we loved him. We had to see it demonstrated in Jesus before we could understand that we needed it. However, once the demonstration had been completed, there were at least two important implications that were then presented to anyone who longed to know God as Father:

Implication #1. If the Father's love is unconditional, it means that he takes the initiative when it comes to love. In almost all of the world's religions, it is the worshipper who must take the initiative when dealing with their deities. In our three years in India, we saw how devoted Hindus were expected to do pujas (prayers) at the many temples around our city as well as in specially designed cupboards hidden away in people's homes. In India, the gods never make the first move, you do (if you know what's good for you). This viewpoint can also work itself into many of the Christian religions that exist around the world. Many Christians believe that they must take the initiative in loving God before he will ever accept and love them in return. Like other religions, they have developed the idea that God must be appeased through church rituals and practices or he will withhold his love and blessing in their lives. However, when we really think through the words of the Apostle John, "This is love: not that we loved God, but that he loved us..." (I John 4:10) it completely changes our view of who must take the initiative. Unconditional love always loves first! An authentic relationship with the Father is not a process that starts with him receiving our love, but with our willingness to receive his! Because God is love, it means that in our first contact with him, we don't encounter anger or judgment, or indifference, but that most basic part of his character – love!

Implication #2. If the Father's love is unconditional, it means that nothing can separate us from that love. One of the most radical passages to be found in the New Testament are the words of the Apostle Paul in Romans 8:38-39 where he said, "I am convinced that neither death nor life, neither angels nor demons, neither the present nor the future, nor any powers, neither height nor depth, nor anything else in all creation, will be able to separate us from the love of God that is in Christ Jesus our Lord." In his relationship with God, there was something about the Father that Paul was absolutely convinced of – that nothing could separate him from his love! At first glance, most Christians would agree with that statement, but in this passage, Paul wants us to see how deeply radical this idea really is. So, he makes a list. He writes a detailed list of all the things in the universe that cannot stand between God's children and his love. It's quite a list.

1. "Neither death nor life." Think about that for a moment. There is nothing in this life that can hinder in any way the Father's ability to love us. No circumstance or situation in our lives; no tragedy or humiliation that might come has any power over his love! If that weren't enough, Paul then doubles down by saying that even death itself has no hold over Father-love! When you consider the most elemental powers that are in our universe, life and death must be near the top of the list, yet even they have no power to alter his love in any way!

2. "Neither angels nor demons." In our ranking of the greatest entities that exist in the universe, these two must surely be in first place: angels and demons. From the pages of the Old Testament right through to the New Testament, angels have destroyed armies and leveled cities and proclaimed great messages from God – but they have no power over love! Even fallen angels, who certainly have no love for the human race, cannot shift even a particle of the Father's love for us. This fact took away a lot of the fear that I once had concerning the demonic realm. I realized that, although I will always have to struggle against principalities and powers, I can do it from a place of complete safety in the Father's love. We should never be cavalier when it comes to the devil, but we

can take great comfort in the fact that there are certain things in our lives that he will never be able to touch!

3. "Neither the present nor the future." Paul now gets even more radical in his list of things that cannot separate us from love – there is apparently nothing I might do in the present or the future that can separate me from that love! It's at this point that many of us discover just how *conditional* our understanding of love really is. Back in the 1980s when I would teach this message around Southeast Asia, I would ask my students to use their imagination for a few moments. I would say to them, "Let's pretend that after our class, I am taking a walk in the neighborhood around our school. After a few blocks, I notice that the door of the local grocery store is open and there is no one in the store. I see an opportunity, so I go into the store, open the cash register and put all of the money into my pocket. As I am doing this, the owner of the store comes out of a back room, sees what I am doing, and starts shouting for the police. In order to silence him, I grab a bottle of Coke and hit him over the head – a little too hard – for I fracture his skull and he falls, severely wounded, right there on the floor in front of me. The police arrive. I am booked for robbery and assault. There is a great scandal here at the missions training school, my family name is ruined, and I never get to be a teacher (or a free man) again." At this point they are a little shell-shocked and more than a little amused, so I look them in the eyes and ask a very difficult question. "Did any of these actions separate me from the Father's love? Paul said nothing in the present and nothing in the future, so did he really mean that there was nothing that could affect God's love for me?" Most of them are not smiling now, because everyone in the room is thinking, "how could God ever love someone who did something like that?" This extreme example points to a quality of love that is so pure (and foreign to us) that the King James translators chose to use a different word: "charity." God certainly did not love what I did in that imaginary story. There would certainly be consequences that I would pay for the rest of my life – but, according to Paul, God's love for me would remain unchanged. And it is this truth (and only this truth) that would ever enable that hypothetical Ralph to find his way back to forgiveness and restoration. Love without conditions doesn't even look like love in the minds of many, but it is a true expression of a perfect father. Many parents tell me that they will always love their kids, no matter what they might do, and we must see that this is but a shadow of the kind of love that emanates from God our Father! However, Paul's list is not yet complete...

4. "Nor any powers, neither height nor depth." When Paul names powers on high or the authorities of human society, he is pointing out that even the might of a government or a dictator can have no influence on unconditional love! I find it comforting to realize that my politics cannot stand between me and the Father's love. Even if a nation makes every mistake that could be made, God's love for the people of that nation remains unchanged; and this means that there is always a path to national redemption. This, I believe, is the key to loving our enemies: the understanding that their sin might separate them from God's presence, but it will never separate them from God's love. So, if God has chosen to love them without conditions, who am I to do anything less? Christians sometimes confuse the characteristics of God's justice and God's love. They think, "Doesn't loving unconditionally violate God's justice?" It is a fair question, but one that is answered when we realize that justice and mercy live side by side in the character of our Heavenly Father. Justice demands there be consequences to sin, but love makes no demands of the one being loved. Every human being who chooses to separate himself from God throughout his life will most probably find himself separated from God in the afterlife, but that has nothing to do with God's love for him. God still loves those who have chosen to dwell there, even when justice demands that they remain. In his masterpiece, "The Problem with Pain" C.S. Lewis points out that, "There are only two kinds of people in the end: those who say to God, 'Thy will be done,' and those to whom God says, 'Thy will be done.' All that are in Hell, choose it. Without that self-choice there could be no Hell. The gates of Hell are locked from the inside" (C.S. Lewis *The problem of pain*). This is worth considering. Hell is not a construct designed by God because he stopped loving unrepentant sinners – Hell was created by those who demanded separation from him and, in the end, got their wish! Seen this way, hell (eternal separation from God) is actually the mark of just how much God really loves us: a love that gives men and women the complete freedom to choose.

5. "Nor anything else in all creation, will be able to separate us from the love of God that is in Christ Jesus our Lord." Nothing in creation, from the smallest microbe to the largest black hole, can step between his love and us!! Notice here that it is a love that is expressed not in feelings, but in Jesus. It is sometimes easy to write off people who seem indifferent (or even hostile) to him. However, we have a clear promise that nothing can stand between

Jesus, Gods living expression of love, and that individual. Some years ago, I realized that people are much closer to salvation than I had originally thought. There is only a very thin membrane of self-will that stands between a person and eternal life. Salvation is as close as the breath it takes to say, "Come Lord Jesus."

When teaching this topic to students in Southeast Asia back in the 80s, I would always introduce this next element of the Father's love with the following question: "What is the difference between deep love and shallow love?" Anyone who has lived past their teenage years knows that there are different depths to love. Puppy-love (Indonesians call it Monkey Love) is different from newlywed-love, which in turn is different from the love of a long-married couple. But what exactly is the difference? As the students would start to list their ideas on the board, it soon became obvious that things like feelings and emotions were not accurate measurements of the depth of love. Eventually we would find our way to the right answer – the difference between shallow love and deep love is a difference of sacrifice.

His Love is Sacrificial

This way of measuring the depth of love is something most of us understand in the natural world. In World War II, people who gave money to buy war bonds showed a love for their country, but those who gave their lives demonstrated a love that was much deeper. Parental love can be expressed through generosity and provision, but there is a deeper love on display when parents sacrifice their time and career for their kids. In our human experience, the way to determine the depth of love seems to be through this measuring line of sacrifice – but can this be applied to God's love? Many see God as a benevolent supreme being who loves us in a general kind of way but is concerned with much bigger things than our small problems and needs. Yet, when we pull out the yardstick of sacrifice and apply it to what scripture says about his love, we discover a depth that is almost unfathomable! In what is probably the most well-known verse in the Holy Bible we read, "For God so loved the world that he gave his one and only Son, that whoever believes in him shall not perish but have eternal life" (John 3:16). This verse has been flashed in so many sporting events and quoted by so many street evangelists that we have perhaps lost the radical message that it once contained. How deeply does God love us? – *God so loved the world that he gave* — It is when we begin to look closely at this sacrifice that we start to comprehend the true depth of his love. Let's try to answer three questions concerning what, why, and how he chose to give.

1. *What did he give?* "For God so loved the world that he gave his one and only son." The Father could have given a sign in the heavens or a fiery prophet or even an unearthly angel. Any of those three things would have represented an incredible amount of love. But his love was far deeper than that. It was a love that was willing to sacrifice his one and only Son.

Theologically, when Christians say that Jesus is the son of God, we don't mean a literal son created by God. The term "Son" refers to his unique relationship with the Father and his divine nature as God. However, even when we get the theology right, we sometimes miss the point – God so loved the world that he gave of himself! The cross is not just a symbol of God's love, it is the ultimate demonstration of it. That he took upon himself the penalty for our sin; that he chose to be personally involved in giving something as a demonstration of love reveals a depth of love that is truly hard to comprehend! Yet, as deep as that love is, the second question reveals an even greater depth...

2. *Why did he give?* This question is answered when we complete the sentence written in John 3:16, "For God so loved the world that he gave his one and only Son... that whoever believes in him shall not perish but have eternal life." The gift of himself was surely a demonstration of great love, but when we look at why he did it, it gets even deeper! Eugene Peterson paraphrased this verse in The Message to say, "This is how much God loved the world: He gave his Son, his one and only Son. And this is why: so that no one need be destroyed; by believing in him, anyone can have a whole and lasting life" (John 3:16 MSG). A sacrificial love alone would have been pretty deep, but the reason for this sacrifice reveals something even deeper – that no human being needs to ever be destroyed! If we ask God, "Why did you do it?" He answers in the words of II Corinthians 5:19, "For God was in Christ, reconciling the world to himself, no longer counting people's sins against them." It was a sacrifice given for a much greater purpose than forming a religion – it was for the purpose of taking sin off the table! Because of this sacrificial love, no one who comes to God will ever hear him say, "Your sin disqualifies you from being loved by me." Of course, we do have to turn from our old life as part of the process of turning to a new life, but his sacrificial love forever removes sin as a barrier to that reconciliation! In human relationships, the age-old formula has always

been: Problem Solving + forgiveness + Reconciliation = Healing, but the cross has reversed that formula. Now it is: Reconciliation + forgiveness + Healing = Problem solving. In other words, because God is reconciling the world to himself by no longer counting people's sins against them – problems can now be worked out as the result of a reconciled relationship, not as a prerequisite to it! It takes a lot of love to look through the sin and reach out to the person, but this third question takes us deeper still.

3.   *How did he give?* If you think about it, there are probably some things that are far worse than death. As a missionary pastor living in Russia, I always felt that I could give my life for others if that was required – but to suffer for them – this was a much more daunting prospect. If the death of Jesus had been nothing more than a legal loophole satisfying the law that said, "The wages of sin is death" (Romans 6:23), God could have found a much cleaner way to do it! Instead, he deliberately chose suffering as part of the whole sacrificial process! This element of suffering was so important that it was prophesied 700 years before it actually happened! In Isaiah 53:3 it says, "He was despised and rejected by men, a man of sorrows, and familiar with suffering." The cross was not an easy death designed to satisfy a condition of the law, it was a cruel and painful death designed to create extreme suffering! There was no legal requirement that forced Jesus to suffer in his sacrifice, but there was a reason for it – to demonstrate the depth of his love!

I've always been intrigued by this statement about Jesus written in Philippians 2:6-8, "Who, being in very nature God, did not consider equality with God something to be grasped, but made himself nothing, taking the very nature of a servant, being made in human likeness. And being found in appearance as a man, he humbled himself and became obedient to death, even death on a cross." Once God found himself in the body of a man, instead of choosing to be the greatest and most powerful man the earth had ever seen, he chose the exact opposite. He humbled himself and became obedient to death. It's natural to think of humility as having the same meaning as humiliation, so we often miss what humility says about his love. Jesus let down all of his defenses, not considering his equality with God as something to be grasped and allowed death to overtake him – not as an expression of humiliation, but as an expression of the humility of love! Real sacrifice will always contain this element of real humility. When you give, you are emptying yourself; you are voluntarily placing yourself into a position of vulnerability. When you give, you are treating others as though they are more important than your own position or comfort; and that is the very definition of what it means to be humble! God loves humanity so much that he chose to give of himself; not just for those who already loved him, but for anyone who is willing to come to him. He voluntarily chose to humble himself and embrace suffering and death for one purpose – to show us all the depth of his love!

One day, while playing with an artificial intelligence app on my phone, I asked it this question, "What place does humanity have in the vastness of the universe?" Its immediate answer was rather chilling. "Humanity is a very small part of the vastness of the universe. The universe is estimated to be about 13.8 billion years old and has a diameter of approximately 93 billion light-years. Within this vast expanse, the Earth is just one of billions of planets orbiting around one of billions of stars in the Milky Way galaxy, which is itself just one of billions of galaxies in the observable universe" (ChatGPT). The infinitesimal smallness of humanity in the midst of God's universe can have the effect of diminishing our concept of his love. We think, "at the very most, he must only love us as a very tiny part of his creation." Yet, throughout the Old and New Testament, his love is never described like that. Even though Jehovah was a great (and rather intimidating) God to the children of Israel, David understood this about his love: "How precious to me are your thoughts, O God! How vast is the sum of them! Were I to count them, they would outnumber the grains of sand. When I awake, I am still with you" (Psalm 139:17-18). In his intimate (and rather turbulent) relationship with Jehovah, David had this insight that added a completely new dimension to our understanding of the Father...

His Love is individual

Notice that David didn't say, "how precious are your thoughts towards us" but "how precious are your thoughts to me, how vast is the sum of them! Were I to count them, they would outnumber the grains of sand!" This is much more than just a good song lyric; it's important to seriously consider what David was saying here about the Father's love. He declared that if he could count each of the thoughts that the Father had towards him – they would number more than the grains of sand on the seashore! Obviously, there are a lot of grains of sand on even the nearest beachfront, so (according to David) just how much does God actually think about each of us? How does this Psalm translate into our understanding of the flow of time? Back in the 80s, I would ask my students to do a math problem with me, "How many seconds are in an average lifespan of 70 years?" After a few seconds of blank looks, I would invite them to do the calculations with me on the white board:

<u>Number of seconds in 1 year</u> = 60 seconds x 60 minutes x 24 hours x 365.25 days

= 31,536,000 seconds.

<u>Number of seconds in 70 years</u> = 70 years x 31,536,000 seconds = 2,207,520,000 seconds in an average human lifespan.

As we sat and pondered that total on the white board, two things became obvious to the class: One, our lives are such brief affairs! Just a little over two billion seconds and it's over! However, the second implication of that number was even more amazing. We know that even on the smallest of beaches there are easily more than two billion grains of sand. So, at the very minimum, God the Father is thinking about you at least 2,207,520,000 times during the course of our lives. In other words, he is thinking about each of us individually – every second --of every minute – of every hour – of every day of our lives! To really understand Father-love, we must grasp the fact that we are much more important to him than we will ever comprehend. His mind is constantly turning to examine our individual lives with the same loving attention that we bestow on our own children. This is what Jesus was pointing to when he said, "Indeed, the very hairs of your head are all numbered. Don't be afraid; you are worth more than many sparrows" (Luke 12:7). The fact that God knows how many hairs are on our heads is not evidence of how meticulous he is, but of how valuable we are! He loves our personalities and our giftings, but he also loves all of the little things about us: how you smile and how you fix your hair (even how many hairs are in that hairdo).

Knowing God's love is the indispensable first step in making the transition from Lord to Father. There are many Christians who are able to serve God pretty effectively as Lord (you don't have to love the boss to do a good job for him). But to say "Abba Father" the Holy Spirit must give us a revelation of love that is without conditions; that is as deep as his sacrifice, and that is as individual as we are as human beings!

Questions To Consider

1. What kind of love did you grow up with as a child? Was it a feeling or a need or a response? How has this kind of love colored your perception of God's love?

2. As you think about the unconditional nature of the Father's love (that nothing in all creation can separate us from that love) what implications does it show you in your own relationship with him?

3. As you consider the sacrificial nature of the Father's love (what and why and how he gave) what does that reveal to you concerning the true depth of his love for you?

4. As you ponder the individual nature of God's love (that he knows every detail and is constantly thinking about you), how does this change your view of your importance in God's eyes?

His Correction

CHAPTER
03

Back in the 1980s when I taught about the Father-heart of God around Southeast Asia, I would always start the week-long session with the same question: "If you had the power to create your own earthly father – what would he be like?" As I shared in chapter two of this book, there was always one characteristic-- his love – that was at the top of the list, but there was also another characteristic – his correction – that was almost always at the bottom. It didn't seem to matter whether I was in the Philippines or Indonesia or later in Russia, I found that this pattern remained consistent – people struggle to see correction as something good! The reason we struggle is not much of a mystery, correction can be painful and humiliating, and many people have a distorted understanding of what it says about them. Take a moment and ask yourself this question: "When I was a small child, how did I feel when I was punished?" My generation (from the sixties) would answer "I felt a lot of pain" for in those days corporal punishment was still the norm (not only in the home but even in school). Even today, most children are not particularly appreciative of a "time out" or a loss of privileges. The reason is that small children have yet to learn all of the nuances that make up adult life. They live in a black and white world. To their minds, anything that brings pleasure is loving and anything that brings pain is unloving. That is why the indulgent Uncle who comes over every week is so beloved by his young nieces and nephews. He doesn't really participate in the ups and downs of raising them – he only spoils them and never says no! We understand and adjust to this phenomenon when it comes to our kids, but we don't realize that when it comes to God – we often still think like children when we are corrected! A blessing is a sign of God's love, but a painful trial must mean that he no longer loves us. In this chapter, we are going to unpack a very important scripture that is found in the book of Hebrews. It answers three important questions that must be asked in order to understand the Father's correction: 1) Why does God correct us? 2) What does God's correction say about us? 3) What is the result of that correction? Let's dive in.

1. (Hebrews 12:5-6) "And have you completely forgotten this word of encouragement that addresses you as a father addresses his son? It says, 'My son, do not make light of the Lord's discipline, and do not lose heart when he rebukes you, because the Lord disciplines the one he loves.'" Although we don't know the identity of the author of Hebrews, we do know that this letter was written to Jewish Christians who seemed to be in danger of falling away from their core values as believers. The reason for this is stated right at the beginning of the text. "Have you completely forgotten this word of encouragement that addresses you as a father addresses his son?" He then quotes a Proverb that most of them had heard all of their lives, "My son, do not despise the Lord's discipline and do not resent his rebuke, because the Lord disciplines those he loves, as a father the son he delights in" (See Proverbs 3:11-12). It's interesting to note that what caused this instability in their Christian walk was not a problem with their enemies, but a problem with their willingness to receive correction from the Father. They apparently were starting to despise the Lord's discipline and to resent his loving rebuke. In this Proverb that is quoted in the book of Hebrews, there is also a solution to their problem: "do not lose heart when he rebukes you, for the Lord disciplines those he loves" (Hebrews 12:6). Apparently, from the time of Solomon (the author of that Proverb) to the first century author of Hebrews, believers have understood that when we start to resent the Father's correction, it is usually because we have forgotten that...

His correction is an act of love

Even though most Christians would not disagree with that statement, there is still in most of us a little child who would disagree quite strongly! For many people, daddy's correction was not experienced as an act of love, but an act of a very different sort. *It might have been an act of anger.* Dad has been taking it all day at work, and when he walks through the door, the first thing that confronts him are the childish sins you may have committed that day. All of the pent-up frustration and rage is uncorked and poured out upon your head (and other places). Your Father is angry and disappointed in you, and that hurts much more than the spanking itself. *It might have been an act of weakness.* Papa comes home drunk again and hears about what you have done. Correction is needed, but his senses are too impaired to administer it correctly. In your heart you resent the hypocrisy of being punished by someone who has himself sinned against the family. *It might have been an act of rejection.* In moments of anger, parents can say some pretty stupid things to their children. "I wish you had never been born" can be taken back later, but it is never ever forgotten. For some children, every act of discipline is seen not as correction, but as only further evidence of their rejection. *It might have been an act of cruelty.* While receiving the punishment, you start to realize that the penalty far exceeds the crime that was committed. There is a growing suspicion that father is secretly enjoying the dominance and the pain that he is inflicting. In our childhood, discipline can easily be perceived as an act of anger or weakness or rejection or even cruelty, but to make the transition from Lord to Father we must fully grasp the truth that the Father's correction is always and without exception an act of love. It is just as much an act of love as his blessings! However, before you nod your head in agreement with that statement, ask yourself two important questions. First, "How do I respond when the Father blesses me?" I am probably quick to tell everyone in church about it and exuberantly lift my hands during the worship service. For several weeks I am walking about an inch off of the sidewalk, for I have irrefutable proof that the Father loves me! Second, "how do I respond when the Father disciplines me?" I am confidently moving in what I thought was the right direction when - wham! - God slams the door right in my face! Am I quick to tell everyone in church? Can I exuberantly praise him during the worship service, or does my face have the expression that causes people to ask, "Is there something wrong?" While it is perfectly human to sometimes respond this way, it is also perfectly clear proof that we have lost the same principle that the Hebrew Christians had lost – that God always disciplines those he loves! In Proverbs 13:24 (NLT) it says, "Those who spare the rod of discipline hate their children. Those who love their children care enough to discipline them." If God the Father hated the human race, the one sure way that he could destroy it would be to spare the rod! Never saying the word "no" and never punishing or correcting is not a sign of love, but a sign of something that is just the opposite of love! The Father cares for us so deeply that he is willing to take the risk of being misunderstood and even despised, because he understands that correction is the ultimate display of love. The Hebrew Christians were in trouble because they had forgotten that fact about God – but there was also something else they had forgotten...

2. "Endure hardship as discipline; God is treating you as his children. For what children are not disciplined by their father" (Hebrews 12:7). Apparently,

correction is not only an act of love, it is also an indication of something very important about the human race.

His correction is the mark of who we are

In this broken and sinful world, we can see how far the enemy has gone to create a mirror image of this truth. For many people, correction is seen as a mark of who they are not – not good enough and not worthy of love. It's not perceived as an adjustment that leads to a positive outcome, but only as payback for doing the wrong thing. This verse in Hebrews reveals just how wrong that perception is. It declares that when God corrects, he is treating you as he would treat his beloved heir, not his incompetent servant! The writer of Hebrews then doubles down in the next verse by saying, "If God doesn't discipline you as he does all of his children, it means that you are illegitimate and are not really his children at all" (Hebrews 12:8 NLT). The amazing truth is that the act of correction places us into a completely unique category – his lawful and legitimate children! As far as we can tell, God doesn't correct the plants or the animals. He enjoys them and loves their simple lives, but they have no need for correction. They are lower in the order of his creation. Plants and animals operate mostly by instinct and the instructions that are laid down in their genetic code. However, those who are called his children stand in a very different category – beings chosen to be made into his image. We possess a free will and a free hand to create in this world. We can choose to love him, which is the deepest form of love. Correction is the Father's way of adjusting our lives to accomplish the ultimate goal of being made in the image of Christ. It is at this point that many who are reading this book might need to pause and say, "Come Holy Spirit" for we must be cleansed of this idea that correction means God is treating us like failures. Hebrews 12:7 blows all of that away when it declares, "Endure hardship as discipline; God is treating you as his children." Hardship isn't nearly so hard if I can remember that it is the great indicator of who I really am – the child whom he is shaping and training in love! As we unpack this passage in Hebrews, we must internalize that correction is both an act of love and a mark of who we really are, but the next portion is equally important...

3. "Moreover, we have all had human fathers who disciplined us, and we respected them for it. How much more should we submit to the Father of

spirits and live" (Hebrews 12:9). The writer of Hebrews points out the parallels that are found in the natural world. Many have experienced an earthly father who had taken an active part in the development of his children, so we should understand that God the Father also has this desire.

His correction is part of our training

So often, people see the training that comes through correction as behavior that is forced upon them by the threat of punishment. A surprising number of Christians do "the right thing" out of a fear of being thrown into the eternal punishment of Hell. For some, there is the feeling that they are being molded into someone else's vision of what a mature adult should look like. It creates a deep-seated resentment that grows as time moves along. It is also the complete opposite of how God chooses to transform us. In the following verses, let's look at two ways the Heavenly Father uses correction to train us as Jesus-followers.

Training Principle #1: "They disciplined us for a little while as they thought best; but God disciplines us for our good, in order that we may share in his holiness" (Hebrews 12:10). In our childhood, our parents disciplined us for many reasons (some good and some not so good) but God the Father's purpose for correction is a quite unexpected one – that we may share in his holiness! Let us not be too quick to move on from this passage. What did it just say? *God disciplines us for our good, in order that we might share in his holiness!* Many Christians read this passage as though it says, "God disciplines us because of his holiness." We have this idea that because God is holy, he must purge the sin that is in us before he can stand to be around us! But that is not the way a father thinks! According to this verse, the reason he corrects us is that we might share in something incredibly precious that is only found at the very center of his character, holiness. As a young Christian, this was a radical idea that completely changed my understanding of the Christian life – that the holiness of God was not something that removed him far away from me, but something that he wanted to share with me! The word in the Greek *(hagiotēs)* describes God's sanctity and pure holiness, and for that reason, it's not something that we can create within ourselves through good works. It only comes when our character is refined. That process is described in Proverbs 17:3 (MSG) where it says, "As silver in a crucible and gold in a pan, so our lives are refined by God." This is one of those kingdom truths that most would prefer to avoid; the idea that God chooses to refine our lives in a way that is similar to how gold and silver is refined. A process that involves four basic steps: 1) Separating the rocks that don't contain gold from those who do. 2) Melting those rocks in a furnace at a temperature of around 2,100 degrees Fahrenheit (1,150 Celsius). 3) Cleaning the melted gold with a mixture of nitric and hydrochloric acid to dissolve the impurities and precipitate solid particles of gold that can be washed, then 4) Recasting the gold into its proper shape and function. Separating, melting, cleaning, and recasting; doesn't sound like a pleasant process does it? And yet, this is the process that leads to partaking of the holiness of our Father. We have many worship songs about how God blesses us and anoints us with his presence, but where are the songs describing how he melts us in the furnace and anoints us with hydrochloric acid? Yet, that is the recipe for a holiness that looks like his. If I'm honest, I must admit that many times I have said, "Get thee behind me Satan" in situations where I should have been saying, "Thank you Father for loving me enough to refine me!"

Training Principle #2: (Hebrews 12:11) "No discipline seems pleasant at the time, but painful. Later on, however, it produces a harvest of righteousness and peace for those who have been trained by it." This second part begins with one of the greatest understatements to be found in Holy Scripture, "No discipline seems pleasant at the time, but painful." No kidding! Discipline is never pleasant, but it apparently leads to a very important result – a harvest! I like the way the New Living Translation renders this verse, "No discipline is enjoyable while it is happening—it's painful! But afterward there will be a peaceful harvest of right living for those who are trained in this way" (Hebrews 12:11 NLT). There is no doubt that every Christian wants their lives to have a peaceable and fruitful harvest. In the book of Galatians Paul almost guarantees it when he says, "Let us not weary of doing good, for in due season we will reap, if we do not give up" (Galatians 6:9). The difficulty is that we don't understand how a harvest is produced! For years, I believed (and even taught) that for a Christian to be a fruitful tree, you only needed to add "nutrients" to the soil around your tree; meditate on the word, have a consistent prayer life, stay in church, and you will become a big tree with plenty of fruit. I believed that until the day that Jesus gave me a gardening lesson! One morning in my quiet time, Jesus underlined these words in John 15:1-2, "I am the true vine, and my Father is the gardener. He cuts off every branch in me that bears no fruit, while every branch that does bear fruit, he prunes so that it will be even more fruitful." In this verse, Jesus depicts himself as the primary central vine in the vineyard, and all of us as the branches connected to that vine. He names the Father as the gardener, and in his role as the gardener, the Father does two basic things in his garden: he removes the unfruitful branches and prunes the fruitful branches. Modern-day farmers understand this principle. If you only fertilize the trees in your orchard, you will grow big leafy trees, but little fruit. To produce fruit, they must be radically trimmed back at a certain time in the season. The result: a smaller tree but a much larger harvest. Some years ago, while going through a time in my ministry when things seemed to be going in reverse, the Father challenged me with this scripture. He asked in my prayer journal, "Ralph, do you want to be a big tree or a fruitful tree? You can't always have both." We are so trained by the world to see correction only as punishment, that we often don't appreciate the crucial role that pruning plays in fruitfulness. As Hebrews says, "No discipline is enjoyable while it is happening—it's painful! But afterward there will be a peaceful harvest." I am convinced that the Father is asking this same question to congregations in our world today, "Do you want to be a big tree or a fruitful tree?" The tendency of some to measure church growth horizontally (through numbers) rather than vertically (through depth of maturity) have sadly caused many to choose the "big tree" option. As a pastor is reported to have once said, "My church is a mile wide but only an inch deep." Could it be that the missing key to Christian fruitfulness today is not found in increasing the fertilizer but by embracing the pruning shears? It is important at this period in the history of the church to realize that although there will certainly be times of pain and difficulty for Christians, the *reason* for those times is not that God is angry with his children. In Romans 5:9 it says, "Since we have now been justified by his blood, how much more shall we be saved from God's wrath through him." This is speaking about more than the outpouring of his judgment in the last days, it is declaring that the Father is not mad at us; we have been saved from God's wrath through Jesus! The Father's correction declares, "I love you and you are my child; I will do everything possible to make you fruitful and to share with you my holiness!"

Questions to Consider

1.   Take a moment and look back at the times that you were punished as a child. How did you feel? Have those childish feelings influenced your reaction to your Heavenly Father's correction in your life?

2.   If the Father's correction is always an act of love, is it possible to see his correction in the same light that I see his blessings? For that to happen, what needs to change in my inner portrait of Father?

3.   What label did correction place upon you in your childhood? Are you willing to ask the Holy Spirit to remove that false label and replace it with one that declares you are his beloved?

4.   What does the phrase "sharing in God's holiness" mean to you?

5.   Can you name a time when you made the choice to be a big tree instead of a fruitful tree? Are there some potentially fruitful areas in your life that needs to be pruned back for a season?

His Provision

The most common denominator that is found in every human and animal species is – provision is part of parenthood. In human beings, the manner and quality of that provision has a strong influence on how we perceive our parents. My father was a good provider according to the standards of the 1950s and 60s. Sometimes the cost of that provision meant that we only saw him late at night, but in my family, we never lacked for anything. An unexpected element of that provision came when I turned the age of sixteen. One evening at the supper table, Dad announced that during my summer break he was going to give me a job in the construction company that he managed. Since it would be a grown-up job paying grown-up wages, I had no problem with that plan. My father's company was responsible for most of the major bridges and interstate highway systems being constructed in the state of Alabama in the 1960s. As I looked forward to the summer, I could imagine myself as a steely-eyed bridge man (complete with hardhat and yellow vest) fearlessly climbing around the bridge that would span the intercostal waterway in Southern Alabama. However, when summer came, I found myself the youngest (and white-est) member of what was (somewhat contemptuously) called "The Root Picking Crew." My expectations fell from Bridge Builder to Root Picker! It is a little-known fact in road construction that when the earthen roadbeds are being built up in preparation for paving a highway, every trace of organic material (like roots) must be removed by hand. If it isn't done properly, the roots will decompose and cause the highway to sag over time. Our job every workday morning was to crank up our old flatbed truck, put it in the lowest possible gear and (without a driver) walk slowly beside it, picking up roots and throwing them into the truck bed. It was backbreaking but essential work. Later in life, I realized my father's wisdom in giving me the lowest job in the company. He was the Vice President of the firm and could have easily given me a job on the bridge crew, but he knew the *kind of provision* that his privileged middle-class son really needed. During the next two summers I developed a strong work ethic (and a strong body) but more importantly, I developed a love and respect for the average working man that has never left me. I picked a lot of roots during those two summers, but I also gradually formed into the kind of adult my father wanted me to be.

We can see this same kind of wisdom in our Heavenly Father when we look at eyewitness reports of his provision in the Bible. One of the most instructive accounts can be found in the Book of Exodus. Most Christians are familiar with the story of how Moses freed his people from slavery, parting the Red Sea and leading them out of Egypt. Over the years, Hollywood has created some exciting images of what that must have looked like, but the movies have never told the complete story of what it was like as they journeyed through the Sinai Desert. An entire nation of thousands of people found themselves in a place so barren and arid that it could never produce the food (or water) that they would need. There were growing complaints as the people realized their dire condition. There was even talk of returning to the relative safety and stability of slavery in Egypt. In what was an amazingly gracious response to their grievances, the Father said to Moses, "I will rain down bread from heaven for you. The people are to go out each day and gather enough for that day. In this way I will test them and see whether they will follow my instructions" (Exodus 16:4). I've always found this to be an intriguing way of responding to their need. The Father didn't say, "don't worry about being in the desert, I've packed up enough food to get you through the journey." Instead, he deliberately chose to provide in a difficult and unusual way. Like my root picking job, it was provision designed to develop something important in their character. That's why he said at the end of the verse, "In this way I will test them and see whether they will follow my instructions" (Vs. 4). Let's unpack this story in Exodus and see if we can learn some principles about the Father's provision.

Provision Principle #1: We don't always recognize it

(Exodus 16:13-15) "In the morning there was a layer of dew around the camp. When the dew was gone, thin flakes like frost on the ground appeared on the desert floor. When the Israelites saw it, they said to each other, "What is it?" For they did not know what it was." The glory of the Lord had appeared in a cloud the day before and God had promised to give them bread — but when that bread was delivered, they didn't know what it was! They even called it "Manna" which sounds like the Hebrew expression for, "What is it?" The Father could have easily caused bagels to drop from the sky, but instead, he provided in a way they did not initially recognize. Moses had to tell them, "It is the bread the Lord has given you to eat" (Exodus 16:15). I believe that this phenomenon happens a lot more often than we realize when it comes to the Father's provision. We ask him to provide more fruit in our lives and then cry out, "what is it?" when he starts to prune our branches. We ask him for a better job, and then think, "what is it?" when he prepares us for that job by shaping our character. We ask out for a stronger marriage, and then cry, "What is it?" when he uses our mate to sharpen and mold us. A few years into our ministry of church planting in Perm, Russia we made the decision to start a full-time, live-in pastor's school for young leaders from around the country. At that time, a lot of the old Soviet institutions were dying out and one of them, a "Prophylactory" (a retreat center for factory workers) made a deal with us to rent an entire floor for a year. We filled it with young leaders and brought in guest speakers from around the world. It was a success – but it was also very expensive! A few months into the school, we met a visiting American businessman from California who thrilled us by promising to fund the remainder of the project. We were all rejoicing and thanking God for his provision, but when we traveled in California to collect the money, he seemed to have no recollection of his promise! We returned to Russia discouraged and empty-handed. As money started to run out, asking the Father for his provision became a major focus of our prayer time with the students. A month later, our family had to make the journey to Helsinki Finland to renew our visas at the Russian Embassy there. On the way, however, we were devastated to discover that a pickpocket had relieved us of our cash, credit and debit cards! By the time we could reach a telephone, our school account had been completely emptied of funds. Some friends kindly gave us a place to live in Helsinki for a week as we considered what we should do. Our prayers were not pretty: "Lord, what is it? You promised to provide for the school, but the businessman reneged on his promise and a thief has taken away the rest of the money! What is going on?" However, as word went out about what had happened, churches started to contact us with financial pledges for the school. In just a few weeks, not only had the stolen money been restored, we had raised enough funds to pay for the remainder of the school in advance! Looking back, I realize now that God had (of course) always planned to provide for the Leadership School, but it was going to be in a way I could never have imagined and did not initially recognize. I never forgot that lesson.

Provision Principle # 2: It has to be gathered

(Exodus 16:16-18) "This is what the Lord has commanded: `Each one is to gather as much as he needs. Take an omer for each person you have in your tent.' The Israelites did as they were told; some gathered much, some little. And when they measured it by the omer, he who gathered much did not have too much, and he who gathered little did not have too little. Each one gathered as much as he needed." Notice an important but somewhat hidden principle in this verse. The Lord did not command them to bring out their bowls and receive as much as they needed; the command was, "Each one is to *gather* as much as he needs" (Exodus 16:16). Could the Father have caused an omer (about 3 pounds) of Manna to appear in their bowls each morning? Of course. The one who had recently parted the Red Sea could have easily managed a bowl of cereal! It's important to realize that there was great wisdom hidden in the way that the Father chose to provide. Just as my earthly father gave me the hardest job as a root picker, there were also some good reasons behind the fact that the Manna had to be picked up. Let's look at a few:

Reason #1: Gathering is work. Manna is described in the Old Testament as, "thin flakes like frost on the ground" (Exodus 16:14) so it wasn't that easy to pick up! As a former root picker, I can testify that continuously stooping down to pick up something at ground level is extremely hard work! However, we must see that God's motive was not to make life hard – but to give them a part to play in the process. Most parents understand this principle: whether it is picking up toys or receiving an allowance for their chores: when work is connected to provision, it builds character in the one being provided for.

Reason #2: Gathering is humbling. In Deuteronomy 8:3, when Moses looked back on this period in their history, he made a very enlightening statement. "He humbled you, causing you to hunger and then feeding you with manna, which neither you nor your fathers had known." Why was it so important to the Father that they be humbled? No father desires to humiliate his children, but apparently God the Father places a great premium on this thing called humility! The Book of Proverbs declares, "When pride comes, then comes disgrace, but with humility comes wisdom" (Proverbs 11:2). James goes even further when he says, "God opposes the proud but shows favor to the humble" (James 4:6). It's easy to forget that in God's kingdom, people are not transformed by the proud "power-over" systems that seek to control, but by the humble "power-under" systems that seek to serve. It was rather humbling for me (and probably for my father) for people to see the boss's son groveling in the dirt on the root picking crew, but the humility it developed formed a central part of who I would later become. When we go back to that recollection of Moses in Deuteronomy, we see that there was also a third important reason why manna had to be gathered. "He humbled you, causing you to hunger and then feeding you with manna, which neither you nor your fathers had known... to teach you that man does not live on bread alone but on every word that comes from the mouth of the Lord" (Deuteronomy 8:3).

Reason #3: Gathering is instructive. God provided in an unusual way because he had an unusual lesson to teach the children of Israel. For the remaining years of that wandering generation, they would not plant or harvest anything from the desert. All they had was what God supplied each morning. This was meant to teach them what is probably the greatest lesson to be discovered in the Old Testament – man does not live on bread alone but on every word that comes from the mouth of the Lord. Gathering God's provision can indeed be hard and humbling work, but it can also be a teacher of life's most important lesson: we cannot flourish only with man-made Manna, we need the Manna of God's word! Let's go back now to the story of the Father's provision for Israel in the desert, for there is still one very important principle to discover.

Provision Principle # 3: It is often only good for a day

(Exodus 16:19-21) "Then Moses said to them, 'No one is to keep any of it until morning.' However, some of them paid no attention to Moses; they kept part of it until morning, but it was full of maggots and began to smell. So, Moses was angry with them. Each morning everyone gathered as much as they needed, and when the sun grew hot, it melted away."

Laying aside for the moment the fact that on the sixth day they received twice as much Manna (in order to avoid working on the Sabbath) – the amazing truth is that Manna had no preservatives! When some of the people ignored the instructions of Moses and tried to hoard it for the next day, they discovered that it had become an unappetizing mess! His provision was only good for 24 hours. Of course, adding a preservative to Manna would not have been a difficult task for the God who preserves the stars in their orbits, so why did he deliberately choose to leave it out? Let's explore two answers to that question.

First, in this story we can see that people were starting to worry about tomorrow. Some of them were setting aside a part of what they had collected that morning in case no Manna fell the next morning. God could see this too, so in the way he provided – *he made it clear that he wanted them to live within the day.* This points to a kind of thinking that has had a great effect on the way we see the world around us. Examine, for a moment, God's provision in your own life. If you stray too far into the future in your thinking, it will seem as though you'll never have enough to meet all of your expected needs. However, if you look only within the scope of this present day, your perspective changes. "My bank account has more money than I could (with a clear conscience) spend in one day. My cupboard and my refrigerator have more food than I could possibly eat in one day. I have more than enough strength to do what I need to do within this one day." Take any situation in life and look at it from the perspective of a single day and you will discover that you have been abundantly blessed! It's sobering to realize how the nation of Israel might have changed if just one element of the Father's provision had been altered. What if manna had been good for a month? The economy would certainly have changed as entrepreneurs bought up people's excess manna, creating "manna-markets" that determined the price of commodities. Political power would have changed, as politicians began to be influenced by those who controlled the manna-market. People's source of security would certainly have changed. "I've canned fifty containers of Manna, so I have no worries for the next few months." Even religious practices might have changed, with people becoming much more devout around the first of the month during "Manna Season." There was a very good reason why Jesus said, "Do not worry about tomorrow, for tomorrow will worry about itself" (Matthew 6:34). That statement wasn't a feel-good expression like "don't worry, be happy" --- he understood that worrying about tomorrow keeps us from seeing what God has provided for today!

There is also a second reason why the Father left out the preservatives in their daily provision of Manna – *it was apparently very important to God that they remain dependent upon him.* If the manna didn't rain down that morning, they didn't eat that day! We know that God is a good father and that he wants his children to grow into the image of Christ, so why is dependency a part of how God provides? The answer is partially found by examining the concept of *contentment*. Most in our modern culture believe that contentment can only come from one thing – having more. Whether it's more finances for the family or more anointing in our ministry or even more emotion in our worship, we are convinced that we will be satisfied if only we can have a little more! Unfortunately, after a lifetime of accumulating more and more, most people discover that real contentment can never be found that way. God does want us to be content, so in the way he chooses to provide for us there is an alternative to needing "more." In the Book of Philippians, we are given a clue about this alternative. Paul said, "I have learned the secret of being content in any and every situation, whether well fed or hungry, whether living in plenty or in want. I can do everything through him who gives me strength" (Philippians 4:12-13). What was Paul's secret? Did his contentment rely on accumulating more and more in his life and ministry? No, he takes great pains to let us know that he had contentment while living in plenty and in need. His "secret" is stated clearly in verse 13, "I can do everything through him who gives me strength." This is much more than just an inspiring turn of phrase; it gives an important insight into how the first Christians saw the world. In our modern world, it's easy to develop the idea that *Contentment = Having all things from him*. But Paul, after a lifetime of dependency upon the Father had a very different formula: *Contentment = Doing all things through him*. According to Paul, real contentedness is firmly connected to a dependency upon God where all that I need, I seek to find through him! We all have a need for security, but it can never be found through bigger bank accounts and safety nets, it must be found through him. We all have legitimate needs for ourselves and our families, but those needs must be approached through his wisdom and direction, not by taking control of our lives. The children of Israel discovered a very radical truth in their relationship with the Father: that they could be content through him in an environment where they could not possibly provide contentment for themselves.

In this process of knowing our Heavenly Father as provider, there is also a deeper principle than just knowing *how* he provides – *we must also know when he can safely provide*. I've discovered in my own life that I am often quite passive when it comes to his provision. It's easy to embrace popular religious jargon that says, "when there is a need, God will provide." But is that always true in real life? There have been times when I have had great needs (and great pressure emanating from those needs) in my career as a missionary church planter. Sometimes it seemed as though we could focus on nothing more than paying the bills and meeting our financial obligations – and in those times of pressure there was something that I learned about knowing the Father as my provider. Back in Matthew chapter six, before telling his disciples not to worry about tomorrow, Jesus said something that we often only half-understand. "Seek first his kingdom and his righteousness, and all these things will be given to you as well" (Matthew 6:33). We often stress the beginning part of that verse, "Seek first the kingdom" but don't always hear what the second part is saying: "And all these things will be given to you as well." What "all things" will be given? Apparently, all of the things that Jesus had just told them not to worry about! The point is this: there are no conditions to the Father's love, but there are definite conditions to the Father's provision. Seeking first the kingdom is the prerequisite to having all things provided. If this is correct, then the most important question we can ask ourselves is not "where can I seek provision?" but "what should I seek first?" C.S. Lewis once famously wrote, "If we put first things first, we get second things thrown in. Put second things first and we lose both first and second things" *(C.S. Lewis, Letters to Malcom)*. There is such great wisdom in those words. When we get confused about our priorities in life, putting less important things (like our needs) first, we are in danger of losing both first and second things! I am convinced that this is the primary reason why Christians don't have the abundant provision that we were always meant to have. The problem is not God's generosity or his willingness to bless us – the problem is in the way that we order our priorities.

I was saved in 1976, which was the heyday of the so-called "prosperity preachers." At first, I was drawn to the message that proclaimed, "Sow a dollar and God will give you a hundred." As I grew older, I came to reject the idea that financial prosperity was the primary sign of Christian maturity. But in the last few years I've started to rethink what Jesus was actually saying in Matthew 10:29-30. Let's take a second look: "Yes, Jesus replied, and I assure you that everyone who has given up house or brothers or sisters or mother or father or children or property, for my sake and for the Good News, will receive now in return a hundred times as many houses, brothers, sisters, mothers, children, and property—along with persecution. And in the world to come that person will have eternal life." Could it be that the famous "hundred-fold" promise that I heard back in the 70s was actually true? Not a promise that was determined by *how much* you gave, but for *whose sake* you gave? When I give for my sake (with the hidden motive of being blessed) I am doing nothing more than putting second things first in a religious way. But if I am giving for his sake and the sake of the gospel, then I can safely expect and receive provision that is far more than I could ever ask or think!

Provision is such a central part of the role of fathers that it is almost impossible to know God as father if you don't know him as your provider. I believe that our inability to see God in this way is at the root of the extreme busyness that we see in our modern culture today. To see yourself as your sole provider is to take on a job that is far too great for any human being. It dominates the life of a person until there is almost nothing left of his time or his relationships. It's not enough to simply repeat religious platitudes; we need a real working understanding of how this process of provision operates in our relationship with the Father. Just as the social structure of Israel would have radically changed with one little alteration in God's provision of Manna, so our society has radically changed (for the worse) because we no longer know him as our provider. Making the transition from Lord to Father is about much more than having good feelings towards him, it's about learning to receive into our lives all that the Father longs to provide for us.

Questions to Consider

1. If it is true that we don't always recognize the Father's provision when it comes, how does that change our expectations? Can you think of an example of his provision that came in a way that you did not recognize at first?

2. When you ask for God's provision, do you also ask to be shown your part in gathering that provision? Have there been times in your life when you have turned away from God's provision because it was humbling, hard work?

3. If the Father's provision (like Manna) is usually only good for a short time, how does this change your understanding of walking in his provision?

4. Are you in a place where the Father can safely bless you with provision? Take an honest look at your life's priorities: what occupies first place in your life and what occupies second?

His Jealous Heart

05

At this point in the book, we've painted a pretty warm and comfortable picture of our Heavenly Father. His love for us is sacrificial, individual, and even unconditional. His provision is given in a way that not only meets our needs but builds our character. Even his correction is an act of love and a declaration of who we really are in his sight. We have a perfect, living example of these qualities in the life and teachings of Jesus. But what about the picture of the Father that is revealed in the Old Testament? Scholars disagree about the bloodier chapters found there. Was God simply working through the framework of an ancient (and distorted) cultural understanding of the gods (as all missionaries do) or was he really as violent as the Old Testament describes him? It's a profound question and one not easily answered. But still the question remains: can we discover the heart of the Father in Old Testament scriptures?

We have already seen the evidence of his provision as a Father when he rained down Manna in the desert. We know that he led them with a pillar of cloud during the day and a pillar of fire by night. He met with Moses face to face in the Tent of Meeting and promised that same kind of relationship to future generations. However, there is another side to the Father in the Old Testament that most of us find rather terrifying. It is expressed in many places, but perhaps most clearly in the Book of Deuteronomy: "Be careful not to forget the covenant of the Lord your God that he made with you; do not make for yourselves an idol in the form of anything the Lord your God has forbidden. For the Lord your God is a consuming fire, a jealous God" (Deuteronomy 4:23-24). It's tempting to think that Moses was only indulging in a bit of hyperbole when he proclaimed that our God was a jealous God. Yet the amazing (and disquieting) truth is that this characteristic of Jealous is referenced *thirteen times* concerning God in the Old Testament! It's found in the Ten Commandments that he etched onto a tablet of stone in front of Moses on the mountain. "You shall not make for yourself an idol in the form of anything in heaven above or on the earth beneath or in the waters below. You shall not bow down to them or worship them; for I, the Lord your God, am a jealous God" (Deuteronomy 5:8-9). Remarkably, it is even listed as one of the *names* of God found in Exodus 34:14. "Do not worship any other god, for the Lord, whose name is Jealous, is a jealous God." In my years as a "Jesus Freak" we were fond of proclaiming the different names of God as part of our worship service. We would joyfully sing, "Jehovah Jira (provider) you are more than enough for me." or "Jehovah Rapha (healer) you will make me whole." However, I don't ever recall singing, "Jehovah Jealous, you'll consume me." Yet, this name seems to be just as commonplace as all of the other names that God gave himself in the Old Testament. The first time that I was confronted with this title, I tried to deflect the implications by thinking, "surely the Old Testament writers didn't mean jealous. Perhaps it can be translated 'zealous' or some other less intimidating word." However, if you look it up in a Bible dictionary, you discover that it is the Hebrew word, "*qanna*" the common term for jealousy! Back in the day, when a Jewish boy saw his girlfriend with another guy, he felt qanna! There is little doubt that this was an accurate description of God's character, for the Apostle Paul used this same phrase in his letter to the Corinthian Christians when he said, "I am jealous for you with a godly jealousy" (2 Corinthians 11:2). So apparently, there is a feeling that God has for us that is real and authentic jealousy, yet without the sin so often connected to human jealousy. Back when I used to teach this in Asian discipleship schools, I would challenge the students to describe jealousy in a way that didn't include sin. It would take them a little time, but gradually they would start to define jealousy as: "Something that occurs when there is a breach in a relationship; a feeling that one has lost a special place that was once held in the heart of another." There is pain and grief associated with jealousy but there is also a desire to restore what has been broken. We have all probably experienced feelings such as these, but when we attribute them to our Heavenly Father, it's rather a shock to realize just how seriously God treats our relationship with him. When I allow someone or something to take his place, he is jealous over me!

It's an even greater shock to go back and read the full text in Deuteronomy 4:24, "For the Lord your God is a consuming fire, a jealous God." There is a temptation to seperate these two phrases and think, "God is a consuming fire towards his enemies and a jealous father towards his children." However, these two phrases are both speaking about one thing: his heart towards us. I like the way that the Free Bible Version paraphrases this verse, "For the Lord your God is a fire that burns everything up. He is an exclusive God" (Deuteronomy 4:24 FBV). Most of us are much more comfortable with the fiery God that Moses encountered when he was tending his father-in-law's sheep on the mount of Horeb. A fire that burned but did not consume; a fire that could warm you but not burn you. A fire that you could admire and even worship, but one that could be kept at a distance! Yet, to understand his jealous heart we must consider this rather uncomfortable part of his nature – *the closer you come to him, the more he will consume of you.* John the Baptist seemed to understand this when he said in John 3:30 "He must increase but I must decrease." Jesus made this principle clear to the disciples when he said, "Those of you who do not give up everything you have cannot be my disciples" (Luke 4:33). It's obvious that the early church understood this when you read passages like Romans 12:1, "Therefore, I urge you, brothers and sisters, in view of God's mercy, to offer your bodies as a living sacrifice, holy and pleasing to God—this is your true and proper worship." It's interesting that in the first church, true and proper worship was not defined by the skill of the worship leader but by the sacrifice of the worshippers! The Father's jealous heart is not a sinful reaction, he's not bitter or resentful, but it is a desire for first place so strong that everything else must be in second place.

As a pastor, I used to wonder why so many people seemed to reach a plateau in their Christian growth. People would seemingly hit a wall and just grow no further. For years I thought the answer was more Bible study or stronger sermons exhorting them to try harder. I now believe that many people stop moving forward when they realize that they are moving closer to the consuming fire! I've shared in earlier books that when I came to Christ as a 23-year-old hippie during the Jesus revolution, my only real talent was playing the harmonica. I'd discovered years earlier that I had a natural talent for improvisation, and I would regularly "sit in" with different rock and blues bands in the Birmingham area. When I became a Christian in Northern California, it was only a few months before I was a member of a Christian rock band touring (in a small way) around the region. The harmonica pretty much defined how I saw myself in those days. But as I started to grow in my relationship with God, I was surprised to discover that the Consuming Fire wanted me to place more than my drug habit on the alter, he wanted my harmonica as well! At first, I thought that "putting it on the alter" only meant to play music for Jesus, but soon I started to understand that it was the instrument itself that he wanted me to give him. Looking back, I realize now that this was the first milestone in my young Christian walk; the first instance where I would be tempted to come no closer to the consuming fire. Of course, God would continue to unconditionally love me, but the intimacy of my relationship was now dependent on what I was willing to let him consume! After a few weeks of soul-searching, I quit the band and put my harmonica on the shelf. To be honest, a part of me still thought that God would give it right back. Instead, he gave me a gift that was anything but natural to my shy, introverted nature: he gave me the ability to stand before people and teach the word of God. Sometimes when I look back at those years, I wonder what direction my life might have taken if I had not allowed my harmonica to be consumed. God is, if anything, persistent; but I have a feeling that it would have taken much longer for my calling as a missionary church planter to be realized if I had not put my most precious possession in the fire.

If we return for a moment to our text in Deuteronomy 4:24, "For the Lord your God is a consuming fire, a jealous God" we must not only grapple with the fact that the Father is jealous over us, but also the fact that in any relationship – *the jealousy felt by one individual creates certain implications for the other individual!* Back in the day, when our Hebrew boy felt jealous after seeing his girlfriend with another guy, there were certain implications that his girlfriend would now have to face: "Do I remain with him or do I start a relationship with this new guy? Am I willing to occupy that special place in his heart?" In the same way, the jealous heart of God creates certain implications for those who would come closer to him. Let's examine two:

Implication #1: We must eliminate the competition.

When it comes to jealousy, whether it is a Hebrew boyfriend or our Heavenly Father, there is one demand that comes before all the others: "If you want to stay with me you have to break up with him!" We understand this when it comes to committed human relationships, but when you look at the history of the nation of Israel, you realize that this was probably the main stumbling block in their association with Jehovah God. They were constantly embracing the gods of other nations who were in competition with him. From the beginning of their time in the Desert of Siena, they were fashioning a golden calf the minute Moses' back was turned. From one generation to another, they continued to turn to the competition. Human nature hasn't changed much since those days. Neither have the false gods that clammer for our worship. That is why there must be regular times in the life of a Jesus-follower when we ask ourselves: "have I allowed anyone or anything in my life that is in competition with the Father?" For the nation of Israel, the competition was the ancient, enticing gods of their neighbors, but for us, the competition can sometimes be a bit more hidden.

There can be *Places of refuge.* The Oxford Dictionary defines the word refuge as, "A condition of being safe or sheltered from pursuit, danger, or trouble." In other words, a refuge is a place where we go in times of trouble. The problem is that when those times come, it's so easy to find refuge in the arms of the competition! It might be a relationship with a friend or the comfort of a lover or the safety of our parents. It might even be a substance like drugs or alcohol (or ice cream) that I run to during the storms of life. And what makes all of this so confusing is that there is nothing basically wrong with the comfort of friends, or parents, or even ice cream – as long as those things do not replace the Father as our primary source of refuge! When Moses blessed the different tribes of Israel at the end of the Book of Deuteronomy, he made it clear that this was a major part of understanding their relationship with Jehovah. "The eternal God is your refuge, and underneath are the everlasting arms" (Deuteronomy 33:27). This was important because of the basic nature of a refuge: it is not a place to go when times are good, it is a place specifically designed for when times are bad! In Kansas, no one ever goes down into the tornado shelter when the sun is shining; you only go there when a tornado is heading straight for you! Yet, for many Christians, the everlasting arms of God are the last place we think of running to when trouble arrives. Many believers envision God only as a judge or as a rule giver - and who wants to go there when the rules have been broken? Perhaps the greatest weapon in the enemy's toolbox is this picture of God that he holds up to us after trouble comes into our lives. It might be the picture of a Father who is ashamed of you, or a Father who's going to punish you; but the purpose of these false pictures is always the same – to cause you to run in the wrong direction, straight into the arms of the competition!

Another example of the competition might be: *Places of renewal.* One of the most common dangers that we face in our fast-paced lifestyle is that we have a disturbing tendency to burn out! We find, to our horror, that we've used up all of our reserves and we start looking for a place to renew them. In those times, most Christians seldom question just where they should be looking, we assume that a vacation or a few days off will fill up the tank again. Yet, most have had the discouraging experience of coming back from a great and entertaining vacation, only to discover that we are just as burned out as we were before! It's a curious fact of modern-day Christianity that while we might turn to the Father for comfort or direction, we rarely see him as a source of renewal. Isaiah 40:31 plainly says that "those who hope in the Lord will renew their strength. They will soar on wings like eagles; they will run and not grow weary; they will walk and not be faint." We see that promise as beautiful poetry, but in fact, it is a beautiful prophecy coming from the Old Testament's greatest prophet! Isaiah declared that if we will learn to hope in the Lord, we will find in him a place of complete renewal. The key is in what we mean by the word "hope." Many read that verse as though it is saying, "Those who *believe* in the Lord will renew their strength" but the word being used here is *hope*. The New International Version is generally an excellent translation of the original text, but this word in Hebrew actually points to something quite different than just feeling hopeful. It is the word, *"qavah"* which literally means (according to the Brown, Driver, Briggs Lexicon) "to twist, stretch, and be in the tension of enduring or waiting." Perhaps this definition explains why a positive attitude will never keep you from running out of steam. *What is needed is not positivity, but elasticity!* Hoping in the Lord is choosing to be stretched in the tension of enduring or waiting., even when everything within you wants to follow the path of least resistance into vacations and entertainments. This kind of hope is not a passive waiting as we might do in the doctor's office, but an active waiting much as a runner who waits at the starting block for the race to begin. The promise made to those who choose to hope in this manner is nothing less than astonishing: "They will soar on wings like eagles; they will run and not grow weary; they will walk and not be faint" (Isaiah 40:31). This is a kind of renewal that goes far beyond the benefit of a vacation! In fact, if I can run and not grow weary then I will no longer see a vacation as a source for renewal at all! It will become a source for something else such as a stronger marriage or a better appreciation of new cultures and places. The Father truly wants to renew us in every way – but we must be willing to come to him and to wait for it. As stated earlier in this chapter, the jealousy felt by one individual creates implications for the other individual, so let's look at a second one.

Implication #2: We must make him the end and not the means.

The honest jealousy felt by our Hebrew suitor required a new level of commitment from his girlfriend. "To continue our relationship, I need to know that I am not just the means to some other end such as a diversion or a good time. I need to know that loving me is the ultimate goal of your interest in me. Because the state of jealousy has this implication for both parties, we must ask: "just what does it mean to make someone the end and not the means?" In one of his most personal and autobiographical books, *A Grief Observed*, C.S. Lewis shared a hidden motivation he discovered in the months following the tragic death of Joy Davidman, the brilliant poet he had met and married in his later years. He said, "Am I, for instance, just sidling back to God because I know that if there's any road to her it runs through Him? But then of course I know perfectly well that He can't be used as a road. If you're approaching Him not as the goal but as a road, not as the end but as a means, then you're not really approaching Him at all" (C.S. Lewis / A Grief Observed). Lewis made this discovery in a time of intense grief, but it is a discovery that every Christian must make at some point in life – *if we are approaching God as a means instead of as an end, then we are really not approaching him at all!*

This tendency to see God as a means comes through a very subtle shift in how a person relates to God over time. As his child, I know that he wants to bless me, so I come asking for that blessing in times of need or uncertainty. But if I'm not careful, the blessing becomes the goal and God becomes only a means of reaching that goal. Apparently, this shift started to happen pretty early in the first church. In a letter to his young protégé Timothy, Paul warned of, "men of corrupt mind, who have been robbed of the truth and who think that godliness is a means to financial gain" (I Timothy 6:5). Paul understood that if godliness is not a means to God, then it is not authentic godliness at all! The fact is, this shift in how we see God is not limited to blessings. I might be so desperate for healing that God is seen only a means of reaching that goal of health. I might need direction for my future to the point that the prayer "what should I do?" becomes more important than the one I am praying to. Even something as basic as feelings can become an end if I'm not careful. There was a time in my past when I realized that my desire for the joy that I found in worship had become the goal of my morning prayer times. Without realizing it, I had placed God in the secondary role of providing a way to enter into that joy. Let us never forget that our God is a jealous God who will never accept a secondary place in our lives! This is such an important issue in the life of a Christian that it would be beneficial to look at some examples of how we can reverse this process.

First, you will start to see him as the end and not the means when you *remember why you were created.* When reading the creation story in the Book of Genesis, it becomes pretty obvious that everything was created for a purpose. Light was created for the purpose of providing the energy needed by every growing thing. Dark was created to be a balance for the day, providing a time rest for some and a time of activity for others. Vegetation was created to provide food and to replenish the oxygen in the atmosphere. Animals were created to be fruitful and multiply upon the earth. But when it comes to the creation of man, there is a pause in the Genesis story. In that pause, God declares something that is quite astonishing. He said, "Let us make man in our image, in our likeness, and let them rule over the fish of the sea and the birds of the air, over the livestock, over all the earth, and over all the creatures that move along the ground" (Genesis 1:26). In that statement, God gives two clear reasons why we were created. The second reason, "let them rule over the earth" we mostly understand (even if we don't do it very well). However, the first reason, "Let us make man in our image, in our likeness" is something we hardly ever think about. What did God mean when he said that the purpose for which we were created was to be made in his image? Obviously, he wasn't talking about a physical likeness but a spiritual likeness, things like a free will and a creative imagination. But why did he include these things in us and not in the rest of creation? The answer is both simple and profound – love. Of course, the Father loves all that he has created, but for that creation to love him back, it must be given the choice to love or not. Without that choice, there is no authentic love. When someone is forced to love another, there might be an outward resemblance of love, but it is all on the surface. Love that comes from the heart is always a free choice made by someone who has been given the power to love or not to love. This purpose points to what is probably the greatest key in making the transition from Lord to Father – *God created me, first and foremost, to love him, and everything else in my life is meant to be a byproduct of that love.* What does it mean for something to be a "byproduct" of something else? The Oxford dictionary defines the word to mean, "An incidental or secondary product made in the manufacture or synthesis of something else." For example, let's imagine that a businessman decides to build a factory. He has done the research and believes that there are great profits to be made in the plastics industry, so he proceeds to build a factory whose purpose is to make disposable plastic cups. He sets up all of the equipment that is needed to create this product: an extruder which uses great heat and pressure to melt plastic pellets; an injection molding machine that injects the melted plastic into a mold, and so on. As the factory goes into production, our businessman discovers that one of the by-products of making plastic cups is a great deal of superheated steam. Being a canny businessman, he decides to divert this steam into a turbine generator that he's installed next to the factory; selling the electricity being produced to the local power company. But what would happen if our businessman became so infatuated with the production of electricity that he started to ignore the production of plastic cups? Obviously, as cup production declined, so would the byproduct of electricity that was being generated. When the businessman lost sight of the primary purpose of his factory, he lost the byproduct of that factory as well. No manufacturer would be that foolish, but this crude example highlights what I believe is a hidden reason why our Christian walk often seems to decline in its quality and effectiveness. When we forget the purpose for which we were created (to know and love the Father) and focus instead on the byproduct of that relationship (ministry or career or calling) the entire process enters a downward spiral! A pastor works harder and harder (with diminishing results) to create better sermons or larger ministries; not realizing that it is the neglect of his primary calling (to know the Father) that is at the root of the problem. An office worker allows the demands of her job to slowly occupy every part of her day. Quiet times become briefer and times alone with God more seldom. Life starts to lose its flavor, so she throws herself even more into her job; not realizing that the problem is in her priorities. She's forgotten her primary purpose as a Christian, to love her heavenly Father. When we start to remember why God made us in his image, not to do but to love, we gradually begin to restore him as the end and not the means.

There is also a second thing that we should consider when it comes to reversing this process: you make him the end when you *desire, above everything else, to please him.* This sounds pretty basic, but I discovered a few years into my ministry that there was a big difference between desiring to serve him and desiring to please him. I was so consumed with working for God that it never occurred to me whether my work was the thing that most pleased him!

There is a tendency for us to think that it was the preaching of Peter or the missionary travels of Paul that most pleased the Father, but could there have been something else in their lives that pleased him more? Some years ago, as I was following my daily reading plan, plowing through the genealogy of unpronounceable names found in the fifth chapter of Genesis, I made a rather surprising discovery. There is a list that starts with Adam, then his son Seth, then his son Enosh and so on. In each listing, we are told the age of the man was when his son was born and his age when he died. When reading this part of the Bible, I usually would only notice how long people seemed to live in those days. But this time I made a surprising discovery. In Genesis 5:21-24 (NLT) it says, "When Enoch was 65 years old, he became the father of Methuselah. After the birth of Methuselah, Enoch lived in close fellowship with God for another 300 years, and he had other sons and daughters. Enoch lived 365 years, walking in close fellowship with God. Then one day he disappeared, because God took him." Of all the luminaries to be found on this list, only one person had a birthday but no deathday – Enoch. The Bible says that he went straight to the Father! He must have been one of the most amazing people in all of the Old Testament. Yet, apart from a prophecy of his quoted in the book of Jude (Jude 1:14-15) there is only one other place in the Bible where he is mentioned. In Hebrews chapter eleven we are given a catalogue of the great men of faith in Bible times, and surprisingly, Enoch is there. "By faith Enoch was taken away so that he did not see death, and was not found, because God had taken him; for before he was taken, he had this testimony, that he pleased God" (Hebrews 11:5 NKJV). You would think that a man with faith so great that he cheated death would have had a "testimony" of being a great miracle worker or a great preacher. However, the one thing that was passed down from generation to generation; the one (and only) thing that constituted his testimony was this, "He pleased God." I sometimes wonder what my testimony will be in the years after my own passing. Will it be, "Ralph was a good Bible teacher" or "Ralph could play a mean harmonica." I'm starting to realize in my senior years that the greatest testimony is not one that focuses on accomplishments, but on the motivations of the heart: "He sought to please God." It's interesting that the first church seemed to have a deeper understanding of this than we do today. In his letter to the Ephesian Christians, Paul points to this idea when he says, "For you were once darkness, but now you are light in the Lord. Live as children of light... and find out what pleases the Lord" (Ephesians 5:8-10). Apparently, living as children of light was less about finding out what would please people and more about finding out what would please the Father! This means that the example we have in Enoch is something we should take very seriously. How exactly do you find out what pleases God? When you look at scripture, you realize that there are many ways to answer that question.

First and foremost, it is probably *love* that pleases God the most. In John 15:12 Jesus said, "This is My commandment, that you love one another as I have loved you." It's interesting that this particular commandment was not that we should love him, but that we should love one another. There are a lot of reasons why we Christians attempt to appear loving to others: for some it is only a duty, while others see love as part of a strategy to build a church – but is it possible to love (even the unloving) simply because we know that it pleases God?

According to scripture, there is also a second thing that seems particularly pleasing to God: *generosity*. In 2 Corinthians 9:7 it says, "Each of you should give what you have decided in your heart to give, not reluctantly or under compulsion, for God loves a cheerful giver." God doesn't simply approve of cheerful giving; he really loves it! It gives him a pleasure that other things in our lives may not. I might give generously if there is a serious need or if there is serious pressure from my peers to give, but what would happen to my generosity if I knew that the Father was "tickled pink" every time I gave?

Perhaps a third example of what pleases God can be found in Romans 12:1 where it says, "offer your bodies as a living sacrifice, holy and pleasing to God." *Sacrifice*. We cannot earn God's blessings when we offer ourselves as a living sacrifice, but we certainly please him when we choose to try. The phrase "living sacrifice" seems to suggest that we are choosing to give more than the dead sins of the past, nut even the living things that define us as individuals. That is pleasing to God!

"For the Lord your God is a consuming fire, a jealous God" (Deuteronomy 4:24). Because jealousy is so mixed with sinful reactions in the world of men, it is easy to overlook how vitally important this characteristic is to our understanding of God the Father. As amazing as it may seem, he really does want to occupy first place in our lives. He actually is jealous over us when we allow other things to dwell at the center. He is determined to help us understand that if we approach him as a means instead of an end, we are really not approaching him at all.

Questions to Consider

1.   If it is true that God sometimes feels jealousy in the relationship you have with him, what does that tell you about the nature of that relationship?

2.   Have there been times in your life when the "consuming fire" nature of God has kept you from coming any closer? Can you list some abilities and talents that you are unwilling to bring to the fire?

3.   When times of trouble have come into your life, can you think of some false places of refuge you have attempted to shelter in?

4.   When burnout has occurred in your life, can you think of some false places where you sought to be renewed? Is it possible to redefine what it means to hope in the Lord?

5.   Can you think of some examples in your own life where you (perhaps without realizing it) treated the Father as a means instead of an end?

His Kingdom

06

Since the title of this book is "From Lord to Father" it might seem a little strange to include a chapter called: "His Kingdom." Isn't talking about his kingdom just going back to the old Lord-relationship? While it is true that salvation must always begin with the acknowledgement that Jesus is Lord, there is a level of intimacy in our relationship with the Father that can only come out of our understanding of his kingship. These days, we don't think a lot about kings and kingdoms, but Jesus, in his teaching on prayer, clearly linked together these two concepts of Father and King to present us with a totally new concept of God – The "Father-King." He said, "This then is how you should pray: our Father in heaven, hallowed be Your name. Your kingdom come; your will be done on earth as it is in heaven" (Matthew 6:9-10). If we are instructed to pray, "Our Father... your kingdom come" then our Father must indeed be the king of that kingdom! Many people struggle with this connection because of the bad examples that we have in the Bible of both fathers and kings. There were fathers like Jacob who had favorites among his sons and Kings like Rehoboam who led his nation into civil war. Even those who operated in the dual role of king and Father (like David) didn't always succeed in personal relationships. There was, no doubt, a great deal of abuse in bible days, but we cannot deny that the biblical role of a father is to provide leadership for his family; in much the same way that a good king leads his people. In fact, it was this trait that qualified a person to be an elder in the early church. In his letter to Timothy, Paul said concerning deacons, "He must manage his own household well, with all dignity keeping his children under control with love, for if someone does not know how to manage his own household, how can he care for God's church?" (I Timothy 3:4-5). Paul made it clear that a father must manage his family as well as provide, and this role was a foreshadowing of how our Heavenly Father manages his kingdom. Therefore, in making the transition from Lord to Father we must embrace a picture of God as Father-King. The two roles cannot be separated. For many, however, this seems like an impossible task. How can I merge together a loving father who cares for me and a king who wants to rule over me? Let's explore what it means to know him in this way.

The Father-King does not impose his authority

When it came to authority, most earthly kings in the past made the choice to force it upon their subjects. You were under their authority whether you wanted to be or not. Because we've all read about those types of kings in history, it's easy to let that worldly lens of kingship create a distorted picture of our Father as King. Many Christians diligently obey what they see as the rules of his kingdom, but it is a diligence that is primarily motivated by a fear of offending the authority of the king. When we see God's authority in this way, it subtly begins to change the tone of our relationship until it becomes one of either appeasement or avoidance. I don't want to suffer the consequences of breaking his authority so I either try to appease and keep him pacified by my obedience, or I try to avoid the consequences by staying out of his way. This pretty much characterizes the way that most of the world's religions relate to their gods.

However, the concept of authority is very different when it comes to the Father-King. He certainly has all authority, but the way it operates in our lives is the polar opposite of a worldly king. There is an intriguing scripture found in the Book of Romans that points to this difference: "Don't you know that when you offer yourselves to someone as obedient slaves, you are slaves of the one you obey—whether you are slaves to sin, which leads to death, or to obedience, which leads to righteousness?" (Romans 6:16-17). The late Tom Marshal (author of the book Free Indeed) used to say that he could sum up this verse in three simple words: *Obedience Creates Authority.* In his letter, Paul points out that there seems to be a kind of "spiritual physics" when it comes to understanding authority. When you willingly offer yourself to obey someone (or something) you become the slave of that which you obey. It is your obedience that creates the authority of that person or thing over your life. I lived in the Philippines during a time when this truth was graphically illustrated. My first year of working with the poor in Manila back in the 1980s happened to be the last year of the reign of the dictator Ferdinand Marcos. What was interesting about the end of his rule was that he was not overthrown by the Philippine military or by some other nation. He lost his authority when one million Filipinos flooded the streets of Manila and declared, "we will no longer obey." Their twenty years of obedience had created his authority and their withdrawal of that obedience had removed it! Our Father is a king with all of the authority that the creator of the universe could possibly have – but it is an authority that he chooses to link with our choice to obey!

If you think about it, this kind of authority is very father-like in nature. Once the children are grown, the only authority a parent really has over them is what the children are willing to give through their obedience. It's bad parenting to try to force your will over adult children, but you can still have that authority in their lives if they choose to listen and obey. The Father-King never says, "I demand that you obey me, or you will know my wrath." Instead, he says "choose to obey me and you will know my authority." This can be quite confusing for those who see God as a worldly King. Some assume that whatever God wants to do in the world, he will just push it through whether people want it or not. Everything is pretty much seen as being God's will. Others think of God's authority as only commanding things to change in Jesus name. If things don't change, they assume that the problem is probably their (or someone else's) lack of faith. When we begin to transition in our understanding from Worldly King to Father-king we discover that the authority of God in our lives is not a formula, but the natural result of our loving obedience. Jesus was pointing to this in John 14:21(ESV) when he said, "Whoever has my commandments and keeps them, he it is who loves me. And he who loves me will be loved by my Father, and I will love him and manifest myself to him." When we start to realize that the authority of Jesus is manifested in our lives not through compulsion (or even through our faith,) but simply through our loving determination to be obedient, suddenly the way to walking in great spiritual authority is opened wide! The King certainly has great authority over all things, but it is my obedience that establishes his authority in my daily life.

The Father-King rules over heirs, not servants

We understand that in worldly kingdoms, the relationship between a king and his subjects is one of Lord and servant. Historically, kings dominated their kingdoms to the point that their subjects were little more than serfs, dedicated to maintaining and increasing the king's wealth. The Father-King, however, is a very different kind of ruler. In the book of Romans, we are shown one big difference. "The Spirit you received does not make you slaves, so that you live in fear again; rather, the Spirit you received brought about your adoption to sonship. And by him we cry, 'Abba, Father.' The Spirit himself testifies with our spirit that we are God's children. Now if we are children, then we are heirs" (Romans 8:15-17). Notice the beautiful logic presented here: a) God's Spirit adopted us into the King's family b) If we are adopted, then we are legitimate children of the king c) If we are legitimate children, then we are the heirs to his kingdom. We are not servants, we are heirs! And if you think about it, the way that a king relates to an heir is very different from the way he relates to a servant. Let's look at three of those differences:

1. An heir is one who will inherit the kingdom. A big part of a Father-King's responsibility is to make sure that his heirs are ready to successfully receive their inheritance. They must have a good grasp of the rules of the kingdom as well as an understanding of how to protect and expand its borders. The heir must learn how to act like royalty: to serve and inspire the people he one day will lead. He must learn how to live a life that is above reproach, for he is not a private individual, he is a representative of the kingdom. When I understand that I am an heir-in-training, it greatly expands my understanding of why I am here on earth. I'm here to live out a fruitful and productive life, but I'm also here to be trained for that life that is to come! It's understanding that death is not the end of things, but the real beginning of who I am meant to be – an heir of the kingdom!

2. An heir has privileges. Jesus once said an interesting thing to Peter when asked about paying the local taxes. "What do you think, Simon?" he asked. From whom do the kings of the earth collect duty and taxes—from their own children or from others? From others, Peter answered. Then the children are exempt" (Matthew 17:25-26). In order not to cause offense, Jesus went ahead and payed the two-drachma temple tax (in a rather spectacular way) but he also made an important point to Peter: obligations are for subjects, not heirs. Heirs have privileges. This doesn't mean that we are better than those who do not yet know the Father-King, but it does mean that our life as heirs is not an obligation (like taxes) but a gift that has been freely given! This concept of the privileges of heirs goes far beyond taxes. There is a *freedom* we are meant to have; a freedom to take risks and even make mistakes. There is a *provision* we are meant to have; provision that is far above all that we could ask or think. There is a *standing* we are meant to have, one that has nothing to do with our efforts. It is real privilege, but for a very different purpose. In the world, the privileged have the ability to draw apart from the less privileged, but in the Father-King's economy, the privileged have the ability to draw nearer in service to the less privileged. The heirs are not over them but under them!

3. An heir must learn who he really is. We don't always recognize our place as Christians because we don't recognize our position as heirs. In Galatians Paul said, "As long as an heir is underage, he is no different from a slave, although he owns the whole estate. The heir is subject to guardians and trustees until the time set by his father" (Galatians 4:1-2). Paul was making an important point here – an heir might appear no different than the lowest servant, but in reality, he owns the whole place! In the same way, Christians might appear to be no different from other religious folks – but in reality, we will one day inherit the kingdom! That fact, however, is not meant to make us proud, but to appreciate (and operate in) the authority we have in the name of Jesus. Not authority over people, but authority over the one who is the sworn enemy of people. Jesus called him "the prince of this world" (John 12:31). The devil understands (much better than we do) who we really are, and when we stand as heirs and resist him, he will always flee! Like the young child whose father is the king, we usually are ignorant as to who we really are. On the outside, we don't seem any different than anyone else, but when we grow into our relationship with the Father-King, we also begin to grow in our knowledge of how all of creation sees us.

The Father-King does not demand sacrifice, he is the sacrifice

One strong image that we have in the history of kings is that of a sovereign, dressed in royal splendor, receiving tribute from his subjects. Whether it's Pharaoh collecting a fifth of the produce of the land, or the modern-day tribute of one hundred million dollars that is paid yearly to the English Royal family, kings demand sacrifice. When we look through this worldly lens, it's easy to see God as this kind of king. After all, in the Old Testament he demanded regular sacrifices from the children of Israel, so doesn't he still expect that of us? To answer that question, we have to understand the difference in how God is presented in the Old Testament compared to the New. It's easy to have the impression that there are almost two different gods presented in those two different testaments – the difference, however, is not one of personalities but one of *covenant*. The writer of Hebrews explained it in this way. "Day after day every priest stands and performs his religious duties; again and again, he offers the same sacrifices, which can never take away sins. But when this priest had offered for all time one sacrifice for sins, he sat down at the right hand of God, and since that time he waits for his enemies to be made his footstool.

For by one sacrifice, he has made perfect forever those who are being made holy" (Hebrews 10:10-14). In the old system, sacrifices offered day after day would cover sin for a time, but they had no power to take it away. It was only when the king himself established a new covenant and came to take upon himself the sacrifice of sin that we were set free from its power! We begin to see that the Father-King is the exact opposite of a worldly king – he does not demand sacrifice; he chooses to become the sacrifice that sets us free! This aspect of sacrificial Father-love was covered in chapter two of this book, but it is important to see that with the revelation of the Father-King, we start to understand the office of king in a very different way.

When Jesus prayed at the beginning of the Sermon on the Mount, "Our Father in heaven, hallowed be Your name. Your kingdom come" (Matthew 6:9-10), he was not only giving a revelation of the Father-King, but also a revelation of a different kind of kingdom. Jesus talked a lot about that kingdom, but perhaps the most fascinating description can be found in Matthew chapter thirteen where he said (five times) "The kingdom of God is like..." Let's look at each of these five statements and allow them to not only show us the values of the kingdom, but to also continue to describe our Father-King.

The Father-King defers judgment in favor of mercy

(Matthew 13: 24-25) "Jesus told them another parable: 'The kingdom of heaven is like a man who sowed good seed in his field. But while everyone was sleeping, his enemy came and sowed weeds among the wheat, and went away.'" I've always found this to be one of the strangest parables of the values of the kingdom to be found in the Book of Matthew. In the story, a malicious enemy decides to sow weeds in his neighbor's wheat field. When the field hands discover what has happened, they make the very reasonable suggestion that the weeds should be pulled up. However, the owner replies, "No, because while you are pulling the weeds, you may uproot the wheat with them. Let both grow together until the harvest" (Matthew 13: 29-30). In other words, determining which plants are weeds and pulling them up does more harm than good! It's important to remember that this was not a gardening lesson that Jesus was giving his disciples, but a description of how the kingdom works!

So, what does this kingdom value say about the king? It's clear in this parable that the day of judgment will surely come. Jesus ends the story by saying, "Let both grow together until the harvest. At that time, I will tell the harvesters: First collect the weeds and tie them in bundles to be burned; then gather the wheat and bring it into my barn" (Matthew 13: 30). However, that judgment is *deferred* until the harvest time. Unlike the world's view of Christianity, it is not the role of Christians to determine who are weeds and who are wheat. In his mercy, the Father allows them to grow together. This is an aspect of the Father that is almost never understood by non-Christians. As Paul said in II Corinthians 5:19 (NLT), "God was in Christ, reconciling the world to himself, no longer counting people's sins against them." Notice that in the Father-King's value system, reconciliation comes before judgment. It's not that he ignores sin, instead he chooses to defer the judgment of sin in favor of the mercy of reconciliation! So many people assume that they are a "weed" in God's garden and would never be good enough to be reconciled to him. However, the Father-King declares that this is not the season for weed pulling! Anyone willing to come in humility will find that their "weediness" is not being held against them. Only in that place of mercy can we be in a position to be free from judgment. Perhaps this is what James meant when he said, "Mercy triumphs over judgment" (James 2:13). To understand the Father-King is to realize, above all else, that his first response is never to judge. In fact, he deliberately chooses not to hold your sin against you in order to make a way for your relationship with him to be reconciled. He understands that weeding damages the wheat.

The Father-King chooses the small

(Matthew 13: 31). "He told them another parable: 'The kingdom of heaven is like a mustard seed, which a man took and planted in his field. Though it is the smallest of all seeds, yet when it grows, it is the largest of garden plants and becomes a tree, so that the birds come and perch in its branches.'" Notice in this parable that the kingdom is not like a tree that's been transplanted into a garden, but like a small seed placed into a small hole in the soil of that garden. Unlike so many things in the world, great things in the kingdom of God almost always start very small. This kingdom value can be confusing when a person decides to launch into a ministry or career. In the west, we have a tendency to start big with rented halls and lots of promotion. This misunderstanding causes many to give up too soon in their pursuit of his calling. A good example of small beginnings is in the story of the Scottish preacher Oswald Chambers. He is a household name in most western Christian circles and his daily devotional, "My Utmost for His Highest" has sold more than thirteen million copies and has been translated into thirty-nine languages. However, he had no idea that the shorthand notes his wife took and compiled of his lectures would, a decade later, become the most popular Christian book ever published! Chambers was the founder and principle of a small rather obscure Bible college in Scotland and later, at the beginning of WWI, a chaplain with the YMCA in Cairo Egypt. He tragically died there of complications from an appendectomy at the age of 43. He probably saw his life's work as a pretty small seed, but it later grew into one of the largest of garden plants in the decades that followed.

So, what does this kingdom value tell us about the king? When we understand the "Mustard Seed Value" of his kingdom, it begins to change our conception of how the Father-King operates in the lives of his children. One of the great misconceptions about how he operates is the popular idea that "God only helps those who help themselves." Those words are not found in Holy Scriptures, but many Christians live as though they were highlighted in red! What is actually found in the Bible are statements like, "God chose the foolish things of the world to shame the wise; God chose the weak things of the world to shame the strong" (I Corinthians 1:27). Notice that Paul is not saying, "God will be strong when you are weak." He is saying that the Father's *first choice* is the smallest among us! When we start to realize that the one who rules over a kingdom that has small beginnings is actively seeking the smallest, not the biggest, it fundamentally changes our notion of kingship.

Why is his first choice the least? There are probably many reasons hidden in the unfathomable wisdom of God, but one obvious reason might be the simple fact that only a dependent relationship with the father-King is of any use to his kingdom. We saw back in chapter four that the provision (Manna) given to Israel in the desert could have been delivered in many different ways, but the Father deliberately gave it in a way that would teach them the importance of dependence. It was that dependence upon God that would define them as a people, and it is still required of his people today. The great tragedy of the modern church is that many Christians are deeply ashamed of being small – not realizing that this is the very thing that God is looking for! He doesn't grudgingly choose the small and the weak, he deliberately chooses them with the understanding that great things always have small beginnings.

The Father-King rules under, not over

(Matthew 13:33) "He told them still another parable: "The kingdom of heaven is like yeast that a woman took and mixed into about sixty pounds of flour until it worked all through the dough." When Jesus started to use this illustration of dough in describing God's kingdom, many probably expected him to say, "The Kingdom of Heaven is like a cookie cutter, pressing down upon the dough to form it into a kingdom shape." Instead, he said that the kingdom is like yeast – It doesn't press down from above but works its way through from within! I believe that this concept of kingdom growth demonstrates why management principles from the business world might grow a church, but not the kingdom. At its core, God's kingdom doesn't grow through "power-over" pressures from the top. Instead, it expands through power-under principles like people coming under other people with grace and love. Ideas like loving your enemy and turning the other cheek were never meant to be clever marketing techniques, they were meant to demonstrate what power-under change really looks like in the Father's kingdom.

So, what does this value tell us about the king? Of course, God is the Lord and ruler of all things. He is sovereign over all that he has created. But the way that he chooses to exercise that sovereignty is very different from the kings of the earth. It only takes a cursory look at the leadership style of Jesus to see that it was completely power-under in the way that it operated. He did not create a new government (or even a new religion). He did not call down angels to deliver him from the Romans. He did not even try to control what his disciples would do after his death, but simply told them to wait for the Holy Spirit, the counselor, to come. Throughout his life and ministry, Jesus made it clear that what they saw in him was an exact representation of what is in the Father. This means that our understanding of how the Father-King rules must radically change if we are to know him fully as Father. When I look at my own history as a Christian, I'm amazed at how often I assumed that God would respond to situations like an earthly king: operating in a power-over manner. In the past, I've asked him to intervene and crush those that I considered enemies. I've expected him to overrule bad situations and force them into the direction that I thought they should go. After all, he is the conquering king, isn't he? I realize now that although it is true that God can do anything he wants, what he wants most is to not violate the free will he has given human beings! This doesn't mean that he just ignores what we are doing, but that he chooses to demonstrate his authority under us instead of over us. Paul was pointing to this when he said in Romans 8:48, "We know that in all things God works for the good of those who love him, who have been called according to his purpose." Notice that Paul didn't say God was over all things, forcing them to work for our good, but that he was within all things, working to mold us into his image! Sometimes, we expect God to change things the way a dictator might change the law – when what he desires is to change things by changing us! Could it be that the proper request in difficult times is not, "Father, change this by your power" but, "Father, change this by first changing me."

The Father-King wants all of our lives

(Matthew 13:44) "The kingdom of heaven is like treasure hidden in a field. When a man found it, he hid it again, and then in his joy went and sold all he had and bought that field." In this section we find a rather unique occurrence: Jesus uses two parables to illustrate one principle of the kingdom. In the next verse he doubles down by saying, "Again, the kingdom of heaven is like a merchant looking for fine pearls. When he found one of great value, he went away and sold everything he had and bought it" (Matthew 13:45-46). Notice in these two parables that, although the treasures are different, the response of the finder is the same: he sells all that he has in order to possess it. It's important to remember here that Jesus is not describing our salvation, but how the kingdom operates. The principle is clear – new life is free, but growth will cost you everything!

So, what does this value tell us about the king? We saw back in chapter five the uncomfortable truth that God is a Jealous God. He has feelings of jealousy without the sin that often accompanies human jealousy. We saw that the Bible goes so far to say in Deuteronomy 4:23-24, "The Lord your God is a consuming fire, a jealous God." It's clear that to posses all that God has for us in his kingdom, we must give all that we have to him! George McDonald the 19th century Scottish author once famously said, "God is easy to please, but hard to satisfy." We are often satisfied just to have God heal a condition, but he will be satisfied with nothing less than complete transformation! Jesus (the one who is the exact representation of the Father) made this very clear when he said, "Whoever wants to be my disciple must deny themselves and take up their cross daily and follow me" (Luke 9:23). To serve the Father-King is to start with the revelation that he wants it all! To me, it is this element of the Father-King's character that presents the most difficulties. It's much easier to create our own personal image of the Father as an indulgent Daddy who demands little of his children. However, when we are faced with a king that wants all that we possess, it requires some sober soul-searching to move any closer! Oswald Chambers, that amazing mustard seed, said it best: "We must continually remind ourselves of the purpose of life. We are not destined to happiness, nor to health, but to holiness. Today we have far too many desires and interests, and our lives are being consumed and wasted by them. Many of them may be right, noble, and good, and may later be fulfilled, but in the meantime, God must cause their importance to us to decrease. The only thing that truly matters is whether a person will accept the God who will make him holy" (Oswald Chambers/My Utmost for His Highest). The Father-King does want to bless and encourage us (after all, we are his children and his heirs) but his highest purpose for us is that we be transformed into his image. The question when coming to God is not, "can I receive it all?" it is, "am I willing to give it all?"

The Father-King draws everyone to himself

(Matthew 13:47-48). "Once again, the kingdom of heaven is like a net that was let down into the lake and caught all kinds of fish. When it was full, the fishermen pulled it up on the shore. Then they sat down and collected the good fish in baskets but threw the bad away." So often in this story, we focus only on the part of that parable where the fishermen collect the good fish and throw the bad away – but that is a function of the fishermen, not the net itself! Jesus didn't say that the kingdom is like a fishing pole, hooking only the chosen ones. He said that the kingdom is like a dragnet: scooping up every kind of fish. The dragnet doesn't differentiate between different kinds of fish, it gathers them all!

When I was a senior in High School, my family moved to the Alabama Gulf Coast. We were fortunate to rent a house next to a beautiful body of water called "Little Lagoon." There was a lot of shrimp in that lagoon, so my father outfitted our small boat with a shrimping net. I had never seen one before and I was fascinated with how it worked. It was a black, inverted-funnel-shaped net with a wide opening attached to two wooden rudders (to keep it submerged and open) with a narrower closed net on the other end. The first time that we dragged that thing around the lagoon, it was a little scary when we pulled it up – for everything that had been in the path of that net had been swept up! Large crabs, and eels and fish with big teeth were all in there, mixed together with the shrimp. That memory always comes to my mind when I read those words of Jesus. The kingdom is like a dragnet that is filled with surprises! I believe that this is a more radical concept than we might realize. The gate is indeed narrow for those who want to follow Jesus, but the net that draws them up to that gate is wide. I think that sometimes we reverse this picture. We see the kingdom more as a lobster trap rather than a dragnet. The lobster goes in through a very narrow door which leads to a larger basket on the other end. However, Jesus said the drawing power of the kingdom is so great that it is like an incredibly wide dragnet sweeping up everything in its path!

So, what does this value tell us about the king? If the kingdom is like a net, then the king of that kingdom is interested in anyone who might be in that net! The separating process at the end of that story, where the good fish are kept and the bad fish are thrown away, must never be seen as an example of God loving only the "good people." It is, instead, an illustration of the consequences of people's choices once they have been drawn in by the net. We must never forget the core of the gospel expressed in II Corinthians 5: 19 which says, "God was reconciling the world to himself in Christ, not counting people's sins against them." That process of being willing to reconcile with people before their problems have been solved is beautifully illustrated by the dragnet in this parable. Good and bad fish are together drawn to him, and anyone willing to turn from self and embrace his Lordship is considered a fish worth keeping. In the way that we see the world as Christians, we must never think of the kingdom of God as an exclusive club where only good people need apply. We must think of the kingdom as a dragnet that is drawing all people to a Father-King who wants to be reconciled with the human race – Jesus is not the gatekeeper; he is the gate, and in the end, it is the free will of the individual that determines who will enter that gate.

When Jesus had finished these parables, he asked his disciples, "Are you starting to get a handle on all this?" When they answered yes, he said, "Then you see how every student well-trained in God's kingdom is like the owner of a general store who can put his hands on anything you need, old or new, exactly when you need it" (Matthew 13:51-52 MSG). I've always thought this was an odd way to end his important teaching on the values of the kingdom; until I moved to Queens New York. My neighborhood looks like something right out of the last century. There are small delicatessens and family-owned businesses – not a big box store to be found! A few blocks away from us there's a small hardware store that has been in that spot for close to seventy years. It's one of those old-fashioned general stores that is packed with things that the owner can place his hand on in a matter of minutes. Anything you might need in the way of hardware he can find. I think it is significant that Jesus chose to close his kingdom parables with that picture. When you are well-trained in God's kingdom and well acquainted with the Father-King of that kingdom, you will (like a storekeeper) be able to put your hands on anything that you might need throughout your life.

Questions to Consider

1. Why is it difficult to think of a father and a king as the same person?

2. If the Father-King rules over heirs, not servants, how does that change your understanding of who you really are as a Christian?

3. If the Father-King does not demand sacrifice, but instead chooses to be the sacrifice, how does that change your understanding of who he really is?

4. Meditate once more on the five kingdom values that Jesus gave us in Matthew chapter 13:

- Weeding sometimes damages the wheat

- All things have small beginnings.

- Power under is better than power over.

- The kingdom is costly

- The kingdom is like a net

If these are the values of the kingdom, what picture do they paint of the Father-King?

The Key to Understanding the Son of God

Jesus has always been my hero. From that summer evening in 1976 when a grubby hitchhiker opened his heart, until now – he has always been my guy! However, the *way* that I see him as a hero has changed over the years. In the beginning, I saw him as the ultimate hippie: the rebel who challenged the religious establishment of his time. As I grew under the loving influence of my Pentecostal church, I saw him as the ultimate miracle worker, healing the sick and giving sight to the blind. Later (for a short while) I saw my hero as the ultimate conservative, calling our nation back to the truths of the Ten Commandments. Jesus is still my hero, but I've discovered that what I value most in his story are not the obvious things such as his power over the enemy or his confrontations with the Pharisees. This change happened some years ago when I was living in the Philippines and teaching regularly in training schools throughout Southeast Asia. In my prayer time, I felt that God was asking me to carefully read through the Gospel of John. As I worked my way through the verses, I discovered that there seemed to be a kind of *pattern* that emerged in the story of Jesus. I realized that I was so dazzled by the miracles and demonic encounters that I had missed what seemed to be the most important lesson that I could learn from his life!

One example of this pattern can be found towards the end of his time with the disciples when he shocked them with the words, "My children, I will be with you only a little longer" (John 13:33). Peter asked, "Why can't I follow you?" (John 13:37). Thomas complained, "Lord, we don't know where you are going, so how can we know the way?" (John 14:5). Philip cried out, "Lord, show us the Father and that will be enough for us" (John 14:8). In his reply to Philip, Jesus said something that can be easily overlooked in our bible reading: "Don't you believe that I am in the Father, and that the Father is in me? The words I say to you I do not speak on my own authority. Rather, it is the Father, living in me, who is doing his work. Believe me when I say that I am in the Father and the Father is in me" (John 14:10-11). In other words, "Show us the Father? Don't you realize that you've been seeing the Father in me this whole time? Every day he has been living in me and doing his work; even my words were not on my own authority!" We all know that Jesus demonstrated what it meant to have a relationship with the Father, but we often don't realize just how *dependent* that relationship really was. That day, as I charted my own relationship with the Father, I began to see that it was actually very linear in nature: My day started with quiet time and then proceeded from one ministry task to another. But if you removed my prayer time from the list, it didn't seem to have much of an effect on the other things that I was doing for God. However, when you look closely at this statement from Jesus, you realize that his relationship with the Father would have been diagramed in a very different way: at the very center would be a circle representing his relationship with the Father – and flowing out of that circle of relationship would come every element of his ministry! If you could somehow remove that central relationship with the Father, you would have almost nothing left of Jesus! For the first time I realized that what set him apart from the other religious figures in the Bible were not his miracles (they happened before and after the life of Jesus); it wasn't his preaching (John the Baptist also drew big crowds). What made him completely different from all the rest was the *kind of relationship* he had with God! His insistence on calling God Father, his repeated statements that his words and deeds were directed by the Father; it was these things that infuriated the Pharisees and even caused some of his own followers to turn away. Before the coming of Jesus there were many powerful men and women of God, but what turned the world upside down was this man who spoke of being in the Father and having the Father in him. I had a kind of epiphany that day: that I would never really understand his ministry for the Father if I didn't understand his relationship with the Father!

In our journey from knowing God as Lord to knowing him as Father, there are really two important milestones that measure our growth. The first is knowing God's father-heart: his love and provision and care over our lives, but the second is equally important – knowing God's father-hood. Webster's Dictionary defines the word fatherhood as, "The state of being a father." In the natural, a man might be a biological father, but that does not mean that he has entered into the state of fatherhood. That only occurs when a man is determined to be a strong and direct *influence* over his children. Jesus did much more than pray "Our Father who art in heaven" – he allowed the

Fatherhood of God to be at the center of every aspect of his life and ministry! It is at this juncture that we perhaps need to address one of the most common misunderstandings that Christians have about Jesus: that he was a special case; the notion that the way he lived his life could never be replicated in an ordinary human being. Throughout the New Testament, it is abundantly clear that Jesus was not an avatar or a phantom but one who was 100% God as well as 100% man. Let's take another look at the important scripture that we touched on in the second chapter of this book. In Philippians 2:6-7 it says, "Though he was in the form of God, he did not count equality with God a thing to be grasped, but emptied himself, by taking the form of a servant, being born in the likeness of men". This passage is not saying that Jesus emptied himself of his divinity, but that he voluntarily stepped into a different paradigm; entering the world of a human being who was born and raised by human parents. He did indeed come to pay the price for our sin, but he also came to be the first fruit of a new generation of human beings. That's why he said to us all in John 20:21 "As the Father has sent Me, I am sending you." In other words, "The way that the Father sent me, the way of a dependent relationship that was central to everything – this is the way that I am now sending you!" After my epiphany that day, I then had a second one: if I'm going to look like Jesus, then my relationship with the Father must look like his! In the thirty-five years that have followed those two revelations, nothing has had a greater influence on my growth as a Christian. So, what does all of this actually look like in the day-to-day life of being a Jesus-follower? To answer that question, let's look at three areas in the life of Jesus that flowed out of the relationship-circle that was right at the center of his life.

1. Motivation for Ministry

This might seem like a strange place to start, but to really comprehend the ministry of Jesus, we must understand that a sense of duty towards mankind was never the primary motivation behind his coming. In the book of John, we get a glimpse of what was. "If God were your Father, you would love me, for I came from God and now am here. I have not come on my own; but he sent me" (John 8: 42). In other words, "It wasn't my idea to come; I didn't feel so responsible over the condition of mankind that I came to save them. I came because, in my eternal relationship with the Father, I was sent!" It is very important to grasp the importance of this, because a sense of responsibility must never be our primary motivation for ministry!

Early in my walk with Jesus, I encountered one of the most unusual missions' organizations in the world: a group called "Youth With A Mission." One of the fruits of the Jesus movement back in the 1970s was that hundreds of recently converted hippies started going on short-term missions' trips organized by a young pastor named Loren Cunningham. As God increasingly used them to bring the gospel to the nations, they realized that you don't have to be a trained professional to reach the world with the good news – you just have to be willing to go! When I encountered them at the beginning of the 1980s, Youth With A Mission had become the largest lay-missions organization in the world. I was impressed. In just a short time I went from working on the production line of an office furniture factory in Leeds Alabama to a missionary training school in Powhattan Virginia. Looking back at that time in my life, I now understand that it was more than a wonderful experience of training and fellowship – it was also very dangerous! Day after day, I was exposed to the tremendous needs of the world. We prayed over remote people groups who had never heard the name of Jesus and learned of the tremendous suffering taking place around the globe. It was good to open my heart to the needs of the world, but the danger was that I might allow a *sense of responsibility* to be my primary motivation for missions. "Just look at all of the poverty in the world today, and here I am living in privilege and comfort. It's my duty to go over there and make a difference!" Although that sounds rather noble, a sense of responsibility can never be enough. If I commit myself to ministry simply because there is no one else to do it, then I am committing myself for the wrong reason and will never find contentment in doing it! YWAM understood this danger and showed great wisdom by requiring a five-month training class that included many weeks of intensive sessions focused on knowing God as Father and listening to his voice. They realized that the prime motivation for going into all the world can never be feeling responsible for the world – it must be a sure sense that the Father is directing you to go. I would later spend the next couple of years living with the poor in the Philippines, and it is certain that I would not have lasted long if my motivation had only been a sense of duty towards the poor.

We see this phenomenon in local church ministry as well. Very early in my walk with Jesus, I was asked by my pastor to be the volunteer Sunday School Superintendent. In our denomination, that meant you were in charge of recruiting teachers and helpers for the Sunday School program. During the announcement time on Sunday mornings, I would put on quite a show describing the great needs of our children; dramatically pouring on as much guilt as I possibly could. I would then pause until some poor soul tentatively raised a hand and said, "Brother Ralph, I will try to help." Unfortunately, within a few months that same person would be again raising a hand to quit in exhaustion and frustration. In private, I was so critical of those volunteers. "What's wrong with Christians today? Is no one willing to sacrifice for our kids?" I didn't realize that the problem was not with them, it was with me! I had failed to recognize that a commitment to any ministry that is motivated by a sense of duty will never last; it has no power to nourish or sustain you!

A good example of this in the New Testament is the time when, after a long journey through Samaria, Jesus and his disciples stopped in a town called Sychar. While the others were getting supplies, Jesus had a life-changing conversation with a Samaritan woman at a public well. Upon their return, they approached Jesus and said, "Rabbi, eat something." What followed was a revelation of where spiritual nourishment really comes from. "I have food to eat that you know nothing about" Jesus said. His disciples said to each other, "Could someone have brought him food?" (John 4: 31-33). In his reply, we hear something that is absolutely crucial if we are ever to understand Jesus. "My food," said Jesus, "is to do the will of him who sent me and to finish his work" (John 4: 34). How often have we ever heard someone talk about doing God's will in this way? Jesus did not say "it is my duty to do his will" he said, "it is my food." It was just as essential to the nourishment of his Spirit as meat and potatoes were to his flesh. If this is true, then we should not be surprised when we (or others) burn out in ministry. Only knowing and doing his will can provide the nourishment we need to go the distance! In an article published by the Baptist International Mission Board entitled: "Five Things That Make Missionaries Leave The Field," – the number one reason was, "Excitement without calling" (Carlton Vandagriff / IMB Newsletter). In modern Evangelical and Charismatic circles, there is so much emphasis placed on having a burden for the world that many young missionaries set themselves up to fail. Burden and emotion alone are not enough. In his timeless devotional, *My Utmost for His Highest*, Oswald Chambers said it this way, "No enthusiasm will ever stand the strain that Jesus Christ will put upon His worker, only one thing will, and that is a personal relationship to Himself which has gone through the mill of His spring-cleaning until there is only one purpose left – I am here for God to send me where He will." It is crucial that we realize this truth: only out of (and dependent upon) our relationship with the Father will we ever be able to complete what God has called us to do. The people that God wants us to serve will not always appreciate us. The folks who welcomed Jesus with Palm branches were demanding his execution just a short time later. Our co-workers will sometimes let us down. Two of Jesus' disciples suggested that they call down fire upon a village that had rejected his message. Later, they argued among themselves about who would be the greatest Yet, you find no record of Jesus being tempted to give up the call – for his motivation flowed out of his relationship as a son, not his duty as the Messiah!

This is such an important point that it bears looking into another example in the New Testament. One of the most popular parables found there is called, "The Parable of the Prodigal Son." We all know the story of the younger son who demanded his inheritance in advance and then wasted it on wild living. We are all familiar with the picture of the Father that Jesus painted in his parable when the son returned and heard his father proclaim, "Quick! Bring the best robe and put it on him. Put a ring on his finger and sandals on his feet" (Luke 15:22). However, the story we don't often hear is the tale of the older son. He had been the responsible one. He had stayed on the farm and had done his work and his brother's work. He was considered a good son by the neighbors and appreciated by his extended family. Yet, when his brother returned and was restored by his father, we get a glimpse into what had been his motivation all along: "The older brother became angry and refused to go in. So, his father went out and pleaded with him. But he answered his father, 'Look! All these years I've been slaving for you and never disobeyed your orders. Yet you never gave me even a young goat so I could celebrate with my friends" (Luke 15:28-29). Centuries later, we can still hear the heart of the older son. He had been the responsible one and had not wasted his inheritance, but he had also grown bitter and resentful of what he had to do around the farm. Notice also how surprised the Father sounds when he says, two verses later, "My son, you are always with me, and everything I have is yours" (Luke 15:31). In other words, "you are always with me, I thought that you were doing this for me!" But he wasn't – his ministry on the farm was not a labor of love for the father, but a labor of responsibility. Notice in this story that the older brother was not just upset about his brother's return, he was also upset with his father. "All these years I've been slaving for you..." Over the decades, I've seen this "older brother phenomena" exhibited in the lives of many responsible people who no longer see their profession or ministry as a labor of love for the Father. A sense of responsibility can easily turn into a feeling of resentment towards the one who has given this heavy burden. To understand Jesus, we must understand the centrality of his relationship with the Father. Even the most basic element of his life, his motivation, came not out of a sense of duty but out of a heart of love. Let's now look at a second area in the ministry of Jesus that must also be mirrored in ours.

2. Resources for Ministry

It was a Saturday morning in the city of Nazareth. Luke tells us that it had been the lifelong custom of Jesus and his family to go to the synagogue on Saturday (the Sabbath). When he entered the sanctuary, there were probably many people who recognized and greeted him; this was the son of Joseph, the local carpenter who worked around town. Every Saturday morning, the order of service in the synagogue was pretty much the same: it would begin with an opening prayer and worship; followed by a reading from the book of the law, and another reading from the book of the prophets; finishing with a short sermon. When the time came for the reading of the prophets, the synagogue leader honored Jesus by handing him the scroll of the prophet Isaiah. As Jesus began to read (and comment) on the text, a very strange thing happened at the end of the service, instead of having tea and bagels in the fellowship hall – the congregation rioted! They pushed Jesus right up to the edge of the hill where the town was built and prepared to throw him off! This has to be one of the most unusual responses to a sermon in the history of sermons! What infuriated the crowd is perhaps a subject for another book, but the powerful and provocative words that Jesus read from Isaiah is of extreme importance on at least two different levels: On the highest level, when Jesus said, "today this scripture is fulfilled in your hearing" (Luke 4:27) he was making it clear that the prophesied Messiah had arrived. However, on another (and equally important) level, Jesus was declaring something very significant about the resources that he would use in the work that would soon be launched. "The Spirit of the Lord is on me, because he has anointed me to proclaim good news to the poor. He has sent me to proclaim freedom for the prisoners and recovery of sight for the blind, to set the oppressed free, to proclaim the year of the Lord's favor" (Luke 4:18-19). Notice that this passage in Isaiah is almost a laundry list of the resources that Jesus would soon draw upon in his ministry: good news to the poor, freedom for prisoners, sight for the blind, deliverance for the oppressed. However, we should notice that right at the top of the list, he also described the *source* of those resources! "The Spirit of the Lord is on me, because he has anointed me" (Luke 4:18). The preaching and the healing and the miracles were not things that were to be found in the natural abilities of Jesus the man. Isaiah plainly prophesied that it was the Father who would anoint him with those things. Just a short time later in the book of John, Jesus again made it clear how important this concept is. "Very truly I tell you, the Son can do nothing by himself; he can do only what he sees his Father doing" (John 5:19). This is the great mystery in understanding Jesus – he could literally do nothing by himself! He certainly could have done everything by himself had he wanted to. He could have healed every lame person at the Pool of Bethesda and delivered every individual that he saw on the street. The deep mystery is that *he deliberately chose to do only what he saw the Father doing.* This means that he was always looking; always drawing closer in his relationship with the Father – for he knew that all of his resources for ministry came only through that relationship!

A few years into our ministry of church planting in the Russian Federation, I seemed to hit a wall when it came to the effectiveness of my preaching. I would prepare what felt like a good sermon for Sunday, but in delivering it, I would consistently struggle in connecting with my Russian congregation. My response in those days was usually to get louder and more dramatic in my preaching style, but nothing seemed to be working. We had started a full-time leadership school in our city, and as I continued to pastor the church full-time as well as lead the school full-time, I entered into what was probably the busiest season of my ministry in Russia. One morning in my quiet time, after a very tiring and frustrating six months, the Father began to gently remind me of something that I had taught others for many years: that the Son could do nothing by himself. I realized that my busyness as a pastor/teacher had lulled me into thinking that I didn't need to be so dependent on my relationship with the Father anymore. This realization led to a time of deep repentance and a major adjustment in how I organized my time each day. As his anointing started flowing back into my messages again, it settled in my mind something that became (and still is) my most cherished life-lesson: that the source of my resources can be found in only one place: consistent time with the Father.

When teaching this subject throughout Southeast Asia back in the 1980s, I would try to get my students to think about what practical resources they needed to do ministry for God. They were in a YWAM Discipleship Training School and had a burden for the nations of the world, but most had little understanding of the resources they would need to reach the world. The schools where I taught were located in places like Thailand, the Philippines and Indonesia, so the students mostly came from situations where there were few resources. "What do we need to go into all the world?" I would ask. After a few lofty responses like, "the Holy Spirit" or "the authority of Jesus" they usually would start to think on a more practical level; listing things like abilities, giftings, vision, and endurance. However, the real challenge in those classes was to try to get them to go beyond seeing what was needed, to seeing what the source of those things was. So, let's take some of these practical resources that we use in ministry and discover how to find them in the Father.

The Resource of Vision

Whether you are pursuing a career or a ministry – it's important to know where you are going! Many people like to set goals for themselves, but so often they are either unrealistic dreams or ideas that are limited by their natural talents and abilities. Even in Christian circles, it's easy for "my vision" to mean nothing more than "my plan." However, when the Bible uses the word vision, such as in Proverbs 29:18, "Where there is no vision, the people perish... " it is using the Hebrew word *Chazown*. This word does not mean a plan or a strategy, but "a dream, revelation, or oracle *from God*" (Strong's Concordance). It might seem rather obvious, but when preparing to do something for God, we must make sure that the vision is from God. When it comes to important decisions, it's critical to understand that our feelings, although important, are unable to provide sufficient proof that the goal is from God. The vision that was set before Jesus was the cross, but in the garden as he agonized over the cup that was given him, it's obvious that his feelings were not in agreement with God's goal. So how can we know if the vision we are following is really one that has been set by the Father? In the next few pages, I would like to give you a little vision test. Not the one that your optometrist gives when you cover one eye and read small letters on a chart, but a series of questions that can help you determine the true source of your vision.

Vision Test - Question #1: Did my vision come from time spent with God?

In my early years as a Christian, I had a tendency to talk about things a lot more than I prayed about them. I soon discovered that my words had the power to create a kind of momentum or current in my life that could easily carry me to places I had not intended to go! In the mid-1980s I had finished planting a church for the poor in the slums of Manila and I was looking for what I should do next. I was a member of our mission's national council, so we pulled out a map of the Philippines and determined that the northern part of the country needed a mission's base. I had been successful in my first attempt, so I volunteered to go north. We recruited some staff and moved to the city of Laoag, which was the capital of the far-northern province of Ilocos Norte. It would turn out to be my biggest mistake in ministry. Within a year I found myself off the mission field and back in America; wounded and desperately trying to pull my life back together. The problem was not that this northern region was more challenging than other places in the Philippines, it was that I had pursued a vision that had come out of brainstorming, not prayer. During that dark night of the soul, I renewed the practice of keeping a prayer journal and recommitted myself to daily accumulating a record of what the Father was saying to me through his word. I had suffered through what can happen when you talk more than you listen, so I determined, from that point on, that every major decision in the future would be based upon what I believed God was saying. It would turn out to be my smartest move in ministry.

Vision Test - Question #2: Is my vision consistent?

While it is true that God will certainly lead us around some unexpected turns in life, the bible promises that he is not the author of confusion (See I Corinthians 14:33 ESV). When ministry or career goals frequently change in a person's life, it might be wise to ask oneself, "is this inconsistency a warning sign that I'm setting my own goals?" After completing my first book (Taking Dictation / 2021 – Notion Press) I started to mentor certain individuals in how to keep a journal of what God was saying. I would always start that process with what I believe to be a fundamental truth about our relationship with God – *what matters is consistency, not quantity.* I have discovered over the years that the people who grow in their ability to hear God are those who spend a small amount of time with God frequently, rather than a large amount of time infrequently. We must never forget that faith is a relationship-centered word. It's not dramatic encounters that build up my faith, but consistent words from the Father that give solid direction and encouragement. I am at the age now where I can look back to several milestones in my life where God gave me a new vision. I spent seven years ministering in the Philippines in the 1980s; eleven years church planting in Russia in the 1990s; ten years pastoring an American congregation in the 2000s and three years in India in the 2020s, writing and serving my wife who was teaching in an Indian University. Each of those milestones started with a new vision, but the formation of each new vision started long before, as we waited for the Father to speak in our prayer journals. I am quite capable of hearing almost anything in my daily journal one time, but when I've heard something dozens of times in the course of many months, I then have the faith to commit myself to that new vision. I love many things about the charismatic tradition, but perhaps its greatest weakness is the tendency to put too much importance on our emotions. I've found that what carried me through the difficult winters in Russia and the challenges of the poor in the slums of the Philippines was not the feelings I originally had when he called me, it was the solid written record of the times that he repeated that call. To say to God, "would you repeat that please?" is not a lack of faith at all – it is the surest way to build up that faith!

Vision Test - Question #3: Is my vision primarily linked to another person?

There is certainly nothing wrong with following the vision of a pastor or a leader – as long as God has given it to you as well! I've noticed in my life that it's sometimes easier to simply follow the vision God has given to someone I admire. "I know that God speaks to that person, so I will just follow what they are doing." Many pastors have groups of people around them who operate in this way; faithful helpers who are working to fulfill the pastor's vision. Unfortunately, this can oftentimes lead to a rather empty and unfulfilling kind of ministry. The work either becomes just another job (or worse) a ministry that is personality-centered rather than God-centered. I believe that the way God builds teams is not through a group following the vision of a leader, but through individuals in a group making the discovery that God has duplicated the vision in their own hearts!

A good example from my generation is the story of the Christian songwriter/singer Keith Green. He was, by far, the biggest star of the fledgling contemporary Christian music world of the 1970s. As his popularity grew, Keith founded an organization called "Last Days Ministries" which had a profound impact upon newly saved hippies like me and my friends. His vision was to see radical young believers sent into all the world and hundreds of people were drawn to follow that vision. Unfortunately, just a few years into his ministry, Keith (along with two of his infant children) died in a tragic plane crash. All who knew and loved him were stunned and grieved over the horrible loss. However, just a few months later, an amazing thing started to happen. The vision that God had given Keith for reaching the world began to be duplicated in the hearts of tens of thousands of young people across the United States (myself included). Mission's organizations were flooded with those who had a personal and driving vision to answer the Great Commission. I've often wondered why God chose to take that amazing musician and visionary at the tender age of 29. He influenced the course of my life more than any other Christian figure of the 1970s and 80s – but perhaps one reason might be that we needed to uncouple our vision from Keith in order to make it our own! Did you pass the vision test? Remember that the purpose of my little test was not to determine whether or not you had a vision for your life, but to discover whether or not that vision came directly out of your relationship with the Father. Let's look now at a second resource that is needed for ministry.

The Resource of Abilities

We saw at the beginning of this section that Jesus started his public ministry by reading, from the scroll of Isaiah, a list of what the prophesied Messiah would do when he came among us: "proclaim freedom for the prisoners and recovery of sight for the blind, to set the oppressed free" (Luke 4:18-19). These were certainly important abilities that he would need, but Jesus understood that for them to work, they had to come from (and be dependent upon) the Father. Unfortunately, this is not how most of us understand the resource of abilities today. We assume that what we should be doing for God is what we do best. An outgoing people-person sees herself a good candidate to be a pastor or elder, while one who's good with numbers sees himself as church treasurer or secretary. We embrace the notion that his strength will make our natural strength richer and more useful in the church or community. However, there was a time in the life of the Apostle Paul when he discovered that *just the opposite* was true!

In his second letter to the believers in Corinth, Paul opened up and shared some surprisingly personal information about himself. He wrote that, in order to keep him humble, he was being afflicted by what he described as a "thorn in the flesh, a messenger of Satan" (II Corinthians 12:7). On three different occasions Paul pleaded with God to take it away. In his reply, God gave Paul what is perhaps the most important principle that we can learn about the resource of abilities: "My grace is sufficient for you, for my power is made perfect in weakness" (2 Corinthians 12:9). The reason why God's grace was sufficient for Paul was not that the Father enjoyed his suffering, it was because the Father wanted to fill Paul with his power – and his power is only made perfect in weakness! Notice the deliberate wording here. God didn't say, "When you are weak, then I will be strong." He said something much more radical: *the place where God's strength is able to work most effectively is in the place of weakness.* In the same verse, Paul made it very clear that he understood what God was saying when he replied, "Therefore, I will boast all the more gladly about my weaknesses, so that Christ's power may rest on me" (2 Corinthians 12:9). Notice that the reason for Paul's boasting about his weakness was not because weakness was pleasant, but for the simple fact that it was the only condition where Christ's power might fully rest on him! Then Paul doubles-down in the next verse by saying, "that is why, for Christ's sake, I delight in weaknesses, in insults, in hardships, in persecutions, in difficulties. For when I am weak, then I am strong" (2 Corinthians 12:10). Think for a moment about what Paul just said – "when I am weak, then I am strong." This idea turns on its head the way we understand serving God. For most of us, any kind of weakness is seen as shameful; something that should be either hidden from sight or improved on in some way. Yet, Paul is declaring that – *weakness is the optimal condition needed to see God's power in our lives!*

I have to confess that for most of my life, I've not looked at weakness as the place to go in times when I needed God's power. I saw it as a place to avoid (or conceal). However, if you think about this principle, you realize that if weakness really is the environment where God's strength is the most effective, then my natural ability is probably the environment where it is the least effective! It's important to stop a moment and really ponder what Paul is implying here: that my strength is the place where God's strength is least effective. This is so opposite to our western idea of "do your best and God will do the rest" that it sounds almost like heresy, but it is, in fact, another key to understanding Jesus. He was saying pretty much the same thing to the Pharisees in the Book of John when he told them, "the Son can do nothing of himself" (John 5:19). The resources that he used in his earthly ministry were not the natural strengths he had been born with; they weren't even the divine abilities he possessed before his birth; they were abilities that came directly out of his relationship with the Father. He deliberately and intentionally chose weakness in order for the power of the Father to work through him! So, how can we, in a real and practical way, learn to do the same thing? At the risk of being repetitive, let's go back one more time to that passage in the book of Philippians that describes the incarnation of Jesus; for in it, we have an illustration of what it means to choose weakness in our own lives. "Though he was in the form of God, did not count equality with God a thing to be grasped, but emptied himself, by taking the form of a servant, being born in the likeness of men" (Philippians 2:6-7). Let's break this statement down into its three natural parts:

Jesus did not hold on to his advantages. (vs. 6) "Though he was in the form of God, [he] did not count equality with God a thing to be grasped..." Paul said that Jesus "did not consider equality with God something to be grasped." I like the way that Eugene Peterson paraphrases this verse in The Message, "Think of yourselves the way Christ Jesus thought of himself. He had equal status with God but didn't think so much of himself that he had to cling to the advantages of that status no matter what" (MSG). Those of us who have certain advantages with our talents and abilities often feel that we have to cling to those advantages when it comes to our ministry or career. We close our eyes to the uncomfortable truth that our strengths are probably the last place where God's power can be perfected. One of the hardest truths of the kingdom is that it doesn't really need any advantages that I might bring from my former life. In fact, those natural advantages can often be a hindrance to what God wants to do through me in the world. I've come to realize that the greatest act of repentance in a Christian's life is not just turning from sin but also turning from the advantages our talents might give us over others. For the majority of us who don't possess any special talents, this is the good news that God's first choice is the foolish and the weak (See I Corinthians 1:27). For the gifted, this is the challenge to deliberately choose not to rest upon our own natural abilities. This doesn't mean that God will not use a person's gifts, it simply means that we cannot cling to them! One of the great paradoxes of God's ways is that you have to die to something before there will be any possibility that it can be used in his kingdom!

Jesus emptied himself. (vs. 7) "... but emptied himself..." When the Bible says this, it is not saying that Jesus ceased to be God, but that he laid down (while on earth) his ability to do things as God. Over and over in the gospels he reminded his disciples, whether it was miracles or teaching or healing, that it was the Father who was doing the work. Because this concept was so crucial in the life of Jesus, I believe that it should also be one of the first steps a new Christian takes: not just bringing sin to the altar, but natural gifts and abilities as well! If this was the first step that Jesus deliberately took as a man, how can we not also take that step as we follow him? I must confess that this presents a very different picture of how to approach Christian training. As a pastor, I spent so much time helping people bring their sin to the altar that I hardly gave a thought towards the idea that they should bring their good stuff to the altar as well! Yet could this (not problem solving) be the great key to having a fruitful and productive life that looks like Jesus? I suspect that it is. The ineffectiveness that we see in the church today is not because the church is filled with ineffective people, it is because of our unwillingness to empty ourselves and intentionally embrace a position of weakness.

Jesus took the form of a servant. (vs. 7) "Taking the form of a servant, being born in the likeness of men." When the Bible says that Jesus took the "form of a servant" it doesn't mean that he pretended to be a servant, like an actor playing a role. It means that he saw servanthood as the most effective position from which to lead and influence the world! Think about that for a moment – in the mind of Jesus, the most influential and history-altering position one could have was not that of a general or a king or a billionaire, but a servant! It is very easy, when looking at Jesus, to miss the fact that he always operated under people, not over them. During the final Passover meal that he would celebrate with his disciples, Jesus shocked them all by bringing out a towel and a bowl of water and proceeded to wash their dirty feet! He then shared this power-under principle of leadership: "You call me Teacher and Lord, and rightly so, for that is what I am. Now that I, your Lord and Teacher, have washed your feet, you also should wash one another's feet" (John 13:13-14). In other words, I'm certainly over you as your teacher and Lord, but I choose to lead you from under your feet, not over your head! We all understand that to have a successful career or ministry, we need certain abilities that we can sow into that career or ministry, but the question is – how do we access those abilities? According to the example we have in Jesus, it is to release your advantages, to empty yourself and to take the form of a servant.

The Resource of Endurance

Back in the 1980s, when I would ask young missionaries-in-training about the resources they would need for ministry it was pretty rare to hear them add the word "endurance" to that list. Most of their energy was directed towards how to get to the mission field, not how to stay there. I don't really know what happened to most of the young Indonesians, Thais, and Filipinos that I taught during those years. However, I know with certainty that all of them eventually came to a place in their lives where they needed the resource of endurance! The problem, however, is that there are two opposite ways that you can do it. You can endure through your own strength or endure through your relationship with the father. Most of us know what it's like to endure in your own strength: to grit your teeth and suck it up and keep moving forward no matter what. The problem with that kind of endurance, however, is that a career or ministry starts to resemble a prison sentence rather than a calling from God!

In 1998, after leading several short-term teams to Russia from our home church in Atlanta, we led a final group of people who, at the end of the outreach, left us in Russia to start a full-time work. We knew that God had called us to plant a church in the city of Perm, but we also knew that the first year we were to strategically pray and systematically study the Russian language. This was a lot harder than it sounds. It was tempting to endure that first year by keeping our eyes on the calendar, counting off the days until we could finally start gathering a church. Around that time, God began to remind me of what I had taught in my Father Heart series for years in the Philippines, drawing my attention to the section known as the "Faith chapter" of the book of Hebrews. There, we are given a glimpse into the kind of endurance that was practiced by two of the most famous people in the Bible: Moses and Jesus. As I looked again at their example of endurance, I realized that to get through that first year, we were going to have to do more than just tough it out. Let's look at how these two individuals developed this resource.

The Endurance of Moses

Most of us know the story of Moses: the child of Hebrew slaves who was adopted by Pharaoh's daughter and raised as a Prince of Egypt. We've read that, as a young man, he became more and more aware of the plight of his people, and (in a moment of nationalistic fervor) killed an Egyptian overseer who was mistreating a Hebrew slave. We know the story of his exile in the wilderness and the moment, standing before the burning bush, when God called him to lead the Hebrews out of Egypt into freedom. What we don't often think about, however, is how this privileged former prince endured forty long years as a goat keeper! When Moses stood before that burning bush, he was no longer a young man. He'd spent most of his adult life isolated out in the fields with his flock. Yet, when God encountered him, he did not find a broken man, worn down by enduring life's difficulties. He found a humble man who was willing to say yes to a call that was much greater than himself. Moses looked pretty good after forty years with the goats! So, what was his secret? In the book of Hebrews, we are shown what it was: "By faith he left Egypt, not being afraid of the anger of the king, for he endured as seeing him who is invisible" (Hebrews 11:27 ESV). Notice that it doesn't say that Moses endured by losing himself in his new job as a shepherd. It doesn't say that he endured because he knew he was being punished for murder. The Bible says that, "he endured as seeing him who is invisible." In other words, the secret to his great resource of endurance was found in *who he was looking to!* What does that mean exactly? Perhaps it means that during those years in the fields, Moses learned how to see the creator through the natural world around him. Perhaps in the silence of those fields he was able to hear that still small voice. We are not told specifically how he did it, but we do know that

the resource of endurance came as a direct result of his ability to see the Father! I've come to believe that it is a mistake to say, "make me stronger Lord" in those times when we are near the end of our ability to endure. A better prayer might be: "help me to see you Lord." Forty years as a shepherd would be a lifetime for most of us, but as Moses endured the wilderness as seeing him who is invisible, he discovered that he was now fully equipped to lead a nation through the wilderness.

The Endurance of Jesus

After pointing to the example that we have of endurance in Moses, the writer of Hebrews now uses chapter twelve to point to the example that we have in Jesus. "Let us run with endurance the race that is set before us, looking to Jesus, the founder and perfecter of our faith, who for the joy that was set before him endured the cross, despising the shame, and is seated at the right hand of the throne of God" (Hebrews 12: 1-2). When I was a child, a relative gave me one of those massive King James family Bibles that you see in most bookstores. This Bible attracted me because it was filled with beautiful full-color illustrations of different parts of the Word of God. It had extremely graphic pictures of Jesus on the cross, and I remember wondering, in my childish understanding, how anyone could possibly endure such brutal punishment. We sometimes imagine Jesus hanging serenely on a polished cross as he finished his work and breathed his last – but the cross was a bloody and humiliating way to die! How did he endure it? It's easy to think that it was out of duty or out of his own divine strength, but the writer of Hebrews shows us how he got through it: "Who for the joy that was set before him [Jesus] endured the cross" (Hebrews 12:2). Notice the similarities here with the endurance of Moses: there was something in front of him; something he was looking to that drew him through the torture of the cross. Over the years, I've observed that most people have a choice in how they are going to get through a difficult situation. There are some who get from the beginning to the end simply by being driven through that time; the expectations of others and their determination to serve God drives them through that difficulty that had to be endured. Most manage to get through it, but they are so wounded and traumatized that it makes them very hesitant to ever face difficulties again. However, there is a second choice that people can make when it comes to endurance, the one that Jesus modeled for us on the cross. He was drawn through that time of suffering by the joy set before him! There was, in front of him, the deep joy that he found in his relationship with the Father; something so real and beautiful that it caried him through the equally real pain and humiliation of the cross. Early on in my career as a missionary, the Lord challenged me with that same choice. There came a time in those years when I experienced a deep betrayal by someone very close to me. As I struggled in how to go through it, the Father said to my heart, "Are you going to be driven by duty or drawn by joy?" Because this is such a crucial question, perhaps we should look a little deeper into what it means to be drawn by joy.

To be drawn, there must be something pulling you. It might seem obvious, but in mountain climbing, I can't tie a rope around my waist and expect the person behind me to pull me up the cliff! He must be in the front and firmly connected to me. I've come to realize that it's not enough for me to say, "I am a Jesus follower." I might be a believer, but to be a follower I must learn to place him in the front and connect myself to him by meditating daily upon his word. To be an effective Jesus follower, I must become someone who is being drawn by the one I am following. When the Bible says, "for the joy that was set before him [Jesus] endured the cross" it wasn't referring to the joy of finally getting off this planet. It was the joy of knowing that his daily communion with the Father was about to be greatly expanded and that he would soon, once again, sit down at his right hand! Throughout the ministry of Jesus, the Father was always at the front, drawing him to the next assignment and the next person he wanted to heal. It wasn't superhuman strength that enabled Jesus to endure the betrayal and the humiliation and the suffering of the cross – it was his lifelong practice of being drawn by the joy set before him!

Joy has the greatest power to draw you. In life, there are many things that can drive you, but only a few things that can draw you. The expectations of others, the demands of a job, even our own insecurities can be powerful forces that drive us through the difficult patches of life, but no one really likes being pushed around! Most would agree that it is far better to be drawn through a difficulty than to be relentlessly driven through it. When we start to look around for what might have this drawing power, we find that it can pretty much be summed up in one word – Joy. The joy of loving and being loved. The joy of discovering beauty and creativity and wonder. The joy of realizing that God sees us as his precious and irreplaceable creations. Joy can draw us through difficulty in a way nothing else can. It has this power because, if you think about it, joy is the ultimate goal of everything God would do in our lives. Jesus said in John 15:11, "These things I have spoken to you, that my joy may be in you, and that your joy may be full." He didn't say, "I have spoken these things that your knowledge may be full" but, "that your joy may be full." Paul said, "For the kingdom of God is not a matter of eating and drinking but of righteousness and peace and joy in the Holy Spirit. Joy stands right alongside righteousness and peace as one of the pillars of God's Kingdom! C.S. Lewis, the academic and atheist who became one of the greatest Christian thinkers of our time, titled the book about his conversion "Surprised by Joy." In a letter to a friend, Lewis later described joy's ability to draw us: "All joy emphasizes our pilgrim status, it always reminds, beckons, and awakens desire." (Letters of C.S. Lewis / New York: Harper, 1966). In other words, joy has a way of reminding us that we are only pilgrims passing through this life. It invites us to move forward as our desire for it awakens. That is the drawing power of joy!

Being drawn by joy is a dynamic process. Someone once said, "Burnout is not about giving too much of yourself, it's about trying to give too much of what you do not possess." Being drawn by joy is not a one-time experience that will draw me through every difficulty in every part of my life. It is a dynamic progression of being filled with joy, giving it away to others, and then being refilled anew as you move towards the source of all joy. When the resurrected Jesus said to the discouraged Peter, "Do you love me? Then feed my sheep" (John 21: 17) he understood that what Peter was facing could never be conquered through duty alone. That is why he linked "do you love me?" with "feed my sheep." It was the most important thing that Peter would ever know as he started ministry on his own – that the joy of our love for Jesus must turn into nourishment for others. Peter realized that day that his motivation to feed the sheep could never be simply because they were hungry, it had to be a dynamic process of loving, giving and then being filled with joyful love again.

The greatest challenge to any ministry of career is not just getting there – but staying there! So often we ask God for the resources that we need to perform a task, not realizing that he also wants to equip us with the resources we need to stay with that task. As the writer of Hebrews said, "Therefore, since we are surrounded by so great a cloud of witnesses, let us also lay aside every weight, and sin which clings so closely, and let us run with endurance the race that is set before us, looking to Jesus" (Hebrews 12:1-2). To try to run with endurance in any other way will eventually cause us to drop out of the race!

Let's go back now to that chart I used to make in my Discipleship Training classroom. The one that had a big circle labeled "Relationship with the Father" and showed how each area in the life of Jesus flowed out of and was dependent on that relationship. For there is a third very important segment of the life of Jesus that flowed only from that circle of relationship.

3. Identity in ministry

For much of my Christian life, I considered talk of "finding your true identity" to be nothing more than secular psychobabble. As far as I was concerned, being a born-again Christian was all the identity that I needed. What I didn't realize until years later was that the question of identity (how you see yourself) is so important that it was actually the main focus of Satan's attack on Jesus at the beginning of his ministry! In each of the three temptations presented to Jesus in the wilderness, the issue was not religious theology – but how he saw himself! In the first temptation, Satan challenged Jesus to prove who he was by turning stones into bread. In the second temptation, Satan again challenged him to prove who he was by throwing himself from the roof of the temple. In the third temptation, Jesus was tempted to prove he was the king by accepting Satan's shortcut to ruling over the kingdoms of the world. We must see the significance of this time in the wilderness, for it was a crucial battle over *where* Jesus would acquire the resource of identity! When you think about it, you realize that this issue of identity is still a primary weapon that Satan uses against human beings every day. The American Heritage Dictionary defines the word identity as, "The set of characteristics by which a thing or person is definitively recognized or known." Unfortunately, that "set of characteristics" was more easily defined in past centuries than it is today. In the past, how a person saw himself was determined in many ways by family, society and tradition. "Who am I?" was an easier question to answer in the first century. In this century it's much harder, and as a result, there is a marked crisis of identity in the lives of many modern people, including Christians. As he does in any crises, Satan tries to take advantage of this uncertainty by tempting us to anchor our identity in something other than God. That "something" might be our personal appearance or our bank account or the kind of work we do; as long as it's not the Father, he is content. He understands (from personal experience) that if anything other than God is placed at the center of our lives, it will eventually lead us into darkness and despair. So, throughout our lives he tries to connect who we are with anything other than our Father. Here are a few examples.

"You are what you do." After seven years of ministry in the Philippines in the 1980s, there was a series of events that eventually brought me and my adopted Filipino son back to the United States. As we got settled into life back in America, the Lord challenged me to consider taking on a very

different kind of career: caring full-time for my ninety-year-old grandmother! We had always been close, and she was at a point in life where she could no longer live alone. My family presented the idea that we would sell her house and use the proceeds to pay me to take care of her at my house in Alabama. As a young man, I had worked a few years in a nursing home, so it made sense. I prayed about it and felt the Lord said "yes" so I took on the job. In the following three years, however, I also took on a lot of confusion over who I really was. Without realizing it, I had so anchored my identity in being a missionary in the Philippines that I didn't know who I was back in Alabama. I used to dread going to church functions where a newcomer would ask me the question that all guys ask each other: "what do you do for a living?" The honest answer, "well, I take care of my Grandma" was not so easy to say in a "manly" way! It was a humbling period in my life, but gradually I began to learn how to put my Heavenly Father in that central anchoring place where I had allowed missions to dwell. Once that process was complete, God was faithful to eventually reissue his call to the nations and later I served for eleven years as missionary church planters in the Russian Federation!

You are how you look. We live in a consumer-culture today that places great emphasis on how you look. Millions go into ad campaigns that have one basic message: "you must look good (free of wrinkles, blemishes, and excess weight) in order to find yourself. The fact that so many of the "Beautiful People" in the movie industry have miserable personal lives is quietly swept under the rug. There is nothing wrong with going to the gym or doing what is needed to look the best you can, but if my outward appearance is the anchoring point of who I am, I will eventually discover (with age) that I have set myself up to fail. Most "mid-life crises" have less to do with our circumstances than with our looks.

You are who we say you are. In the three years that we lived in the southern part of India; it was surprising to see the power that Indian families have to shape the identity of their children. My wife taught English in an all-women's university and as we got to know many of her students, we could see that most of them had little control over the direction of their lives. In a culture where arranged marriages were still the norm, many candidly admitted that the purpose of their education was not to pursue a career, but to make them more attractive marriage partners to the right kind of men (chosen by their parents). Family exerted tremendous pressure over every aspect of their future and anchored them to the life-message, "you are who we say you are." While it is easy to give in to that kind of control in our attempts to honor our father and mother, we must see that even family relationships can turn dark if they are what determines who we are. I find it interesting that even Jesus was faced with this pressure when he entered his hometown and heard his neighbors saying, "isn't this the carpenter's son?" (Matthew 13:55). They took offense that he dared to be someone other than what his place in his family declared him to be.

How we see ourselves as Christians is one of the great determining factors in how we will see God's plan for our lives, so how do we resolve this question of identity? The answer is both simple and challenging – we fix our eyes on Jesus (See Hebrews 12:2). Not believing in Jesus or having faith in Jesus but fixing our attention on what we know of his life here on earth. One of the most important things that we know (and often overlook) about Jesus is that he was born into this world. This was by choice, not coincidence, and one of the many reasons why God made this choice was that we might have an example of a perfect human life, from beginning to end! Jesus had to develop as a person in just the same way that you and I developed growing up. Physically, he had to learn how to walk and how to use his spoon – he had to be potty trained! Mentally, he had to learn his place in the family, but also to form his own unique identity as a person. So, as we fix our eyes on Jesus, let's try to also fix our understanding on how he developed the resource of identity as the perfect man.

How Jesus saw himself

After one of the longest journeys that he would ever make in his ministry, traveling more than a hundred miles (by foot) to the region of Caesarea Philippi, Jesus looked around the campfire one night and asked the guys what seemed to be an innocent question: "Who do they think I am?" One by one, the disciples started to talk about the rumors they were hearing around the marketplace. One answered, "Some people believe that you are the resurrected John the Baptist." Another said, "I heard people saying that you were Elijah." A third chimed in, "I heard that they think you are Jeremiah or one of the other prophets of old" (see Matthew 16:13-14). They probably had a quiet chuckle together – but then things got serious. "What about you?" he asked.

"Who do you say I am?" There was probably an uncomfortable silence around the campfire until, finally, Simon Peter answered, "You are the Messiah, the Son of the living God." Everyone waited to see if Jesus would scoff at such an amazing statement. Instead, he said something that was even more amazing: "Blessed are you, Simon son of Jonah, for this was not revealed to you by flesh and blood, but by my Father in heaven" (Matthew 16: 15-17). No one was chuckling now. He looked Peter in the eyes and declared what is probably the most important truth that we can know about Jesus – *he saw himself as the Messiah, but he also saw himself as a Son!*

When you read about the life of Jesus in the gospel record, you realize that he could have found his identity in many different things. Religious people were convinced that he was a prophet, called by God to bring Judaism back into a healthy balance. Political people saw him as a king who would finally overthrow the Roman oppressors. Nearly everyone believed that he was a healer and a miracle worker; the crowds that gathered now were filled with the sick and the needy. Anyone in that position would be understandably tempted to find his sense of self-worth in all of their expectations. Yet, the only response that caused him to say, "God just showed you" was when Peter said two things: his title (Messiah) and his identity (Son). We can be pretty sure that this was how Jesus saw himself, for in the New International Version of the Bible, he referred to himself an astonishing 132 times as "Son." We must realize that this is more than just a "fun fact" about Jesus, it is a critical clue in understanding how he operated (and survived) in ministry. There came a time when the crowds rejected him as a prophet (after being invited to partake of his flesh and blood). Almost everyone would take offense when Pontius Pilate asked, "is this your king?" Yet we find no record of Jesus ever having a crisis of identity! This was simply because his security did not come from who people thought him to be – it was an identity that was fully rooted in his relationship with his Father! Let us also not forget that when Jesus said, "As the Father sent me, so send I you" (John 20:21) he was making it clear that our own identity as Christians must also be developed in the very same way!

So, we come to a very important question in our journey from Lord to Father – how exactly does one develop a primary self-identity as a son or a daughter of the Father? The Apostle Paul, in his letter to the Christians in Rome, gave them a pretty clear pathway that they seemed to have followed throughout most of the first century. Let's take a close look at what he said to them: "Those who are led by the Spirit of God are sons of God. For you did not receive a spirit that makes you a slave again to fear, but you received the Spirit of sonship. And by him we cry, "Abba, Father." The Spirit himself testifies with our spirit that we are God's children. Now if we are children, then we are heirs – heirs of God and co-heirs with Christ, if indeed we share in his sufferings in order that we may also share in his glory" (Romans 8:14-17). In chapter six of this book, we looked at verse 17; how it names us as heirs, not servants, of the Father's kingdom. Now we want to more carefully unpack the entire passage, for it reveals three distinct things that must happen in our relationship with the Father if we are to find our identity in being sons and daughters.

We must learn to be led

"Those who are led by the Spirit of God are sons of God" (Romans 8:14).

It's interesting that in this verse, Paul links two things together that we normally don't connect with one another – our source of leadership and our sense of identity. He didn't say that "sons" are those who believe in the Spirit of God but those who are *led* by the Spirit of God. As I've mentioned in earlier chapters, the source of leadership in Jesus' life is one of the key factors in really understanding him. Over and over, he reminded his disciples that the Son could do nothing by himself; that he could only do what he saw the Father doing (See John 5:19). However, what we don't always see is that this awareness of being constantly led by the Father was a powerful tool that formed how Jesus, the man, saw himself. As he daily paused to see what the Father was doing in people's lives; as he spent time in solitude listening to the Father's voice, it created an unshakable self-awareness of himself as a son; one that was impervious to the expectations of others. Paul was looking to this example that we have in Jesus when he said, "Those who are led by the Spirit of God are sons of God" (Romans 8:14). This is so important that we should probably go a little deeper in answering the question: How can one learn to be led?

To be led requires that you give control to the leader. There is a very subtle change that happens in how you see yourself when you start to believe that you can lead your own life. This change is probably also the greatest barrier to discipleship – for a person unwilling to give up control will find it difficult to follow one who must be in control. Jesus didn't empty himself on a whim. He voluntarily gave up ownership over his life; as we saw earlier in Philippians 2:7, "Not counting his equality with God as something to be used to his advantage." He did this because he understood that only an identity as the Son would equip him to do his ministry as the Messiah. "Not my will but yours be done" were not words of defeat, but words that represented his rule of life! For Jesus, doing the will of God was not some vague ideal, it represented a daily choice to give the Father full control over everything. So often in my own life, I've asked God to give me wisdom or strength when I probably should have been asking him to take control. "Not my will but yours be done" must be the first prayer on our lips at the beginning of each day if we are going to truly learn to be led!

To be led requires that you listen to the leader. In my years as a pastor, I've noticed that, when it comes to being led, there can be a subtle self-deception in the life of a believer. Bob considers himself to be a mature follower of Jesus. When there are times that he is faced with a life-altering decision, he (rightly) sees it as his duty to pray over that decision. So far, this sounds pretty good, but what Bob means when he says he is "praying over" something is that he is letting God know about the situation. The deception in this kind of thinking is the hidden assumption that letting God know somehow guarantees that what happens next will be according to his will. Bob has done his Christian duty to "pray over" this decision, so now the ball is in God's court! It's easy to forget that being led is not informing the leader about the path you are taking – it is hearing from the leader which path you are to take! In many ways, Bob is only putting a religious spin to the old shortcut of being led by circumstances. "I prayed over it and the door opened, so God must be leading me!" In my first book (Taking Dictation/Notion Press) I pointed out that the Bible describes the Father as one who is speaking all of the time; and one of the main ways that he speaks is through his word. When reading the Bible, it's easy to believe, "I've just had a deep insight into this verse" instead of believing, "God has just spoken to me through this verse." Over the years I've become convinced that we hear the voice of the Father in the Bible on a much more regular basis than we realize. The problem is not that he is silent, it is that we take credit for our insights into what he is saying! One of the spiritual practices that has changed my life significantly is that, when I have a fresh understanding while meditating on scripture, I make the decision (by faith) to believe that it is the Father speaking. Naturally, if it is the Father speaking, then I am going to write it down, and note the date, and keep it as a record of what God is saying to me personally. Nothing has helped me more in learning to be led. In 1998, when my wife and I felt that God was leading us to move our young family to the Russian Federation, friends would say, "you are so fearless to be going to a place like that." It was hard to make them see that personal courage had nothing to do with it! We were moving to Russia because, over the course of many months, we had received dozens of journal entries telling us to go! The truth is that it really doesn't require much bravery to go where God is leading – only a willingness to listen and keep a record of what the leader is saying.

To be led doesn't require that you know the details. If you've ever been part of a tour group, you know that the group doesn't really need to know much about how to get to the final destination. The tour leader knows the route and every stop along the way – you can simply enjoy the journey. We understand this when it comes to a vacation, but we struggle when it comes to our Christian journey. Over the years I've encountered many people who sincerely desire to go where God would lead them – but they are waiting until he shows them both the beginning and the end! Unfortunately, the hard truth about being led by the Lord is that he has a tendency to not give us much advance information. In 1998 we knew that God was calling us to start a church in Russia, but how that would be accomplished wasn't revealed until after we had arrived. In our case, the process required a year of prayer and day-to-day living in the city of Perm before he would show us where and how to start the church. In those days, Russia had not been open very long to the west and well-meaning people would say to us, "you'd better put something together quickly before the door closes." It made sense, but our "heavenly tour group leader" kept saying, "wait and let me show you how (and when) I want to do this." It was tempting to set an arbitrary time limit on how long we would take to plant the church. Everything in me wanted to hang up a white board and outline a three-year plan to establish and release the church. However, I realized early on that since God had not revealed the destination, our attitude would have to be, "we are here for the rest of our lives if that is what it takes." In our case, it took eleven years. Looking back, I can see now that a plan cooked up on a white board could never have foreseen the crisis pregnancy centers that grew out of the church or the leadership training schools that continued even after we left

Russia. It would never have included things like the sister church planted in an autonomous Muslim region nor the Russian missionaries that were sent to places like Tajikistan and China. All of that would have definitely not fit onto a white board! For us, it was much better that we didn't know the details. Most Christians want to have a sense of identity that is rooted in Christ, but they don't always realize that this identity can never come from our church activities – it can only come from our source of leadership. Let's return now to this important passage in Romans 8:14-17 and seek to discover a second principle in how to find our identity in our relationship with the Father.

We must remember how we became sons and daughters

"The Spirit you received does not make you slaves, so that you live in fear again; rather, the Spirit you received brought about your adoption to sonship. And by him we cry, 'Abba, Father'" (Romans 8:15).

Back in the 1980s when I taught around Southeast Asia, I would always ask my class (before reading that scripture) "Do any of you remember exactly *how* you became a son or daughter of God?" For at least five minutes they would call out all of the traditional things that Christians like to say, "I gave my heart to God" or "I prayed a prayer of salvation." To which I would reply over and over, "those are good and important things, but that is not how you became a son or daughter." Eventually, some precious young person at the back of the class would remember the cross and raise a hand. "I am a son because of the work of Christ upon the cross that made it possible for me to be adopted into his family!" It's so easy to forget isn't it? To forget that the position of son or daughter was not obtained at birth or even with a prayer – without the cross there would never have been any adoption!

In 1984 I was part of a small team living in the slums of Manila. We were attempting to plant a church focused on reaching and discipling the urban poor. In those days, the Barrios were desperate places where unemployment was high, and disease was rampant. Along with our fledgling church we also had a small health clinic that focused on preventative medicine and healthcare education. In the Philippines, the most prevalent health crises for the poor in the 1980s was the rapid spread of tuberculosis. The challenge for us was to not only make the medication available, but to also get people to take it on a regular basis. When the medication was taken infrequently, the bacteria had a nasty habit of mutating into a TB-resistant strain, making treatment much more difficult. As a result, we had a steady stream of adults and children coming in daily to receive their medication. One TB patient in particular was an undersized six-year-old with an over-sized personality named Michael. At that time, his family was quite destitute and lived on the street, so he started spending more and more time around our team. We all fell in love with Michael, and as time went on, I started to feel that God was leading me to look into the possibility of adoption through the Philippine system. I did not have the right kind of visa or support to adopt a child, but I did have the enthusiastic agreement of Michael's parents and a miracle-working God who gave me favor with the government. I will never forget the final part of that long process. We went to the courthouse and Michael was issued a brand-new official Filipino birth certificate stating that his name was now "Michael Hale" and that his father, from that point on, would be Ralph Hale. He was, years later, able to reconnect with his natural parents in the Barrio, but that day Michael's life took a completely new direction. He became an American citizen and (to everyone's delight) the first grandchild in the extended Hale family. I discovered that my love (and my family's love) for Michael was no different than if he had been our own blood relation. Now, when I read in the book of Romans, "The Spirit you received does not make you slaves, so that you live in fear again; rather, the Spirit you received brought about your adoption to sonship" I see my adoption into the Father's family in the light of Michael's adoption into mine. I am much more than forgiven; I have been given a new name and a new family! Like Michael, I did nothing to earn that place; I was transplanted into God's family by a power that was much greater than myself! When it comes to our identity as Christians, it is vital not to forget our adoption. Over the years I've noticed that it's tempting to credit my place as "son" to my faithfulness in ministry or my willingness to go into the world. But when I remember how I became a son; it brings back the humility that must be at the core of all that we do as Christians. I became a son not because of what I did, but only because of what Jesus did on the cross. In Romans 8:14-17 there is also a third important element in how we are to see ourselves as sons and daughters:

We must be assured by his Spirit

"The Spirit himself testifies with our spirit that we are God's children" (Romans 8:16).

I like the way the Good News Bible paraphrases that verse. "God's Spirit joins Himself to our spirits to declare that we are God's children" (GNB). Every human being is surrounded every day by competing and even conflicting voices declaring who we really are. The voice of parents: suggesting what we should do with our lives. The voice of circumstances: successes and failures trying to form an image of how we see ourselves. The voice of our culture: declaring that what we do determines who we are. Yet, in the midst of all these voices, we are told that God's Spirit has chosen to join himself with our spirit and declare who we really are – his children! When we think about the role of the Holy Spirit in our lives, there is a tendency to only focus on the gifts or the fruit of the Spirit, but here we are being told that a major purpose of the Holy Spirit is to testify that we are sons and daughters of the Father! Perhaps this is the greatest key to developing a strong sense of identity in him. We can choose to be led by the father and we can choose to not forget how we became his children, but the truth is that what we hear (or don't hear) every day from our heavenly Father is the greatest determining factor in how we are going to see ourselves. Every parent understands that what you declare to your children about themselves will form how they see themselves. God is a father in every sense of the word, and he understands this principle as well. He is daily speaking to each of us about who we really are, the problem, however, is that we're often not listening!

In the Old Testament we have the story of a great man of God who, for a time, had stopped listening. The prophet Elijah had offended the powerful rulers of his country, and as a result, had become filled with fear and self-doubt. He ended up in a cave, complaining to God that he was the only prophet left in the world (see I Kings 19:11-19). The Lord's response was very informative. "Go out and stand on the mountain in the presence of the Lord" (I Kings 19:11). When Elijah did that, he learned something very important about the voice of God. There came a wind so powerful that it literally tore the mountain apart – but the Lord wasn't in the wind. There came an earthquake that shook the very foundations of the mountain – but the lord wasn't in the earthquake. There came a fire that devoured everything in its path – but the

Lord wasn't in the fire. After all of these dramatic exhibitions of the power of God, there came one final thing, "After the fire came a gentle whisper" (I Kings 19:12). As Elijah started listening again to that gentle whisper, he remembered the truth of who he was; that he wasn't the sole survivor; that God had reserved seven thousand people in Israel who had not bowed down to the false god Baal (I Kings 19:19). His amazing record of miracles and messages as a prophet was not enough to keep him from a crisis of identity, he needed God's Spirit to attach himself to his spirit and to declare "you are not alone."

Most Christians think of our "quiet time" as only being a place of prayer for others or a place to receive direction. We don't realize that it is also a place where we fully develop our identity as sons and daughters. I've had a daily prayer journal for more than thirty years now, keeping a record of what I felt God was saying through his word to me. Yet, when I randomly open any of those journals, I discover that so much of what is written there is not instruction but encouragement! God's Spirit assuring me again and again, of who I really am! As I move now into my seventh decade, I've started to realize that this assurance was the real key to being able to take the risk of going into all the world. It wasn't God's instructions that gave me the courage to step out, it was his consistent gentle whisper reminding me of who I am: not a pastor or a missionary – but a son! Changing the way that you see yourself is not a passive process that automatically happens over time, it is a deliberate choice to learn to be led with the knowledge that you have been adopted into his family. It is finding a quiet place where his Spirit can join with your spirit and declare who you really are!

Just how much are you worth anyway?

When you think about how a sense of identity is formed in a person, you realize that this process involves much more than just your relationships with others. Identity is also developed in how you see your *personal value* in comparison with people around you. Most folks, if they are honest, don't really believe their lives are worth all that much. This is actually quite true if we look only at the value of our physical body. 99% of the human body consists of six elements: oxygen, carbon, hydrogen, nitrogen, calcium, and phosphorus. They have a total worth of about $576.00 on the open market.

That doesn't seem like much compared to the cost of things today! Even the average per capita earning of an American ($65,000 a year) doesn't look that impressive (at least in the U.S.). When you add to this a consumer culture where successful people are portrayed as those with beautiful homes and the latest gadgets, you find that we all are bombarded with one blaring message: "you are worthless." Even in our Christian culture, we often measure our value by our spiritual gifts or by a theology that says, "you are a sinner saved by grace." Considering oneself to be valuable can even be seen as vain and worldly in the eyes of many churchgoers. Yet, in contrast to our culture, we find that Jesus had a lot to say about our value. Things like, "Don't be afraid; you are worth more than many sparrows" (Luke 12:6-7), and just a few verses later, "how much more valuable you are than birds" (Luke 12:24). I believe that it's important to ask ourselves – why is this issue of value so important to Jesus? His words describing our value were something more than just an attempt to be encouraging,

he understood that – *the value we place on something will determine how we treat it!* One of my favorite shows on PBS is Antiques Roadshow. For me, the attraction is not the world of antiques but what happens when people discover the true value of the object they've brought in to be appraised. You can see it on their faces; they are thinking, "from now on, you're going to have the place of honor in my house!" In our attempts to anchor our identity in the Father, there may be times when we need to bring ourselves to God's Antique Roadshow, for he is well qualified to show us things about our value that we've never seen in ourselves before.

Our purchase-price. Most believers agree with the concept that Jesus redeemed (purchased back) our lives through his work on the cross – but what did it actually cost him? What was the purchase price? Even though most protestants don't hang a crucifix on the wall of their homes, it can be a good reminder of just how much we cost him! The cross was not something that just happened to Jesus, it was the focal point of his life and ministry. After his resurrection, you can see in the New Testament epistles that it remained a focal point for the early church. In Peter's letter to them he said, "For you know that it was not with perishable things such as silver or gold that you were redeemed from the empty way of life handed down to you from your ancestors, but with the precious blood of Christ, a lamb without blemish or defect" (1 Peter 1:18-19). Notice that he wasn't revealing the price of their redemption – he was reminding them that they were supposed to already know it! Apparently, in the first century church, one of the basic discipleship principles that young Christians were expected to know was that their redemption price was more valuable than perishable things like silver or gold. Notice also that (like Antiques Roadshow) Paul also saw this connection between their perception of personal value and how they treated themselves. In 1 Corinthians 6:20 (NLT) he said, "For God bought you with a high price. So, you must honor God with your body." It's interesting that, to Paul, freedom from sexual sin did not come from will power, but from a revelation of one's purchase price! Honoring the sacrifice that Jesus made for us is meant to be much more than honoring him, it is also meant to honor and recognize our true value which is revealed in that sacrifice.

Our net worth. In the corporate world, the net worth of a business is a number that is constantly fluctuating. Back in the day, the BlackBerry was the very first smart phone on the market, and at its peak in 2008, it was valued at more than 85 billion dollars. It was a huge success and could be found in the pocket of most Americans (including President Obama). Yet sixteen years later, in the age of the iPhone, Blackberry no longer made cell phones at all and had a net worth of just two billion dollars! On a more personal level, The brand-new Toyota Corolla that I purchased a few years back instantly lost 20% of its value as I drove it out of the dealership. My five-year-old iPhone (which still works fine) is now worth 87% less than its original price. Because the net worth of things can so rapidly depreciate, it's easy to believe that this applies to people as well. Many feel that if their productivity diminishes, then their value diminishes as well. The real challenge in changing this kind of thinking is very fundamental – *to reexamine the standard of measurement that I am using in order to calculate my worth.* If I use the world's standard of productivity, it's easy to get a pretty low number, but if I use the kingdom standard of the Father's love for me, I discover that I have a very different price tag! Like the people on Antiques Roadshow, we must realize that it wasn't the functionality of an antique that determined its value – it was how much that object was loved and desired by collectors! This demonstrates the great power of love: it has the ability to create, in the one who is loved, a worth that has nothing to do with productivity. We saw at the beginning of this book that the Father's love is unconditional in nature. The word "unconditional" means that he loved us before we ever loved him, and he has promised that nothing – no sin or circumstance or even a demon from hell – could ever separate us from that love (See Romans 8:31-39). My bad choices might still have consequences in my life, but they have no power to diminish my worth in the eyes of the Father. Much of my poor self-image came through the failures and mistakes I committed early in in life, but when I learned that those mistakes did not diminish his love, my true net worth was revealed.

Our shelf-life. Whether it's the medicine that you buy at the pharmacy or corn flakes at the supermarket, one universal rule is that everything has a shelf life; a limited amount of time it will remain fresh and wholesome. It's very easy to apply that kind of thinking to people, especially when you find yourself in the dreaded "senior" category. Once again, our culture reinforces this by lifting up youth as the main selling point for merchandise and even as the only hope for our future. It is very easy to encounter a crisis of identity as you approach middle and old age. However, what our culture doesn't tell us is that weakness, if used properly, is a great advantage in the Father's kingdom! As I pointed out back in chapter seven, when the Apostle Paul said, "Therefore I will boast all the more gladly about my weaknesses, so that Christ's power may rest on me" (II Corinthians 12:9) he was pointing to what is probably Christianity's best-kept secret when it comes to determining our shelf life – weakness makes room for God's strength! One of the cruelest deceptions that is presented to people who have passed the days of their youth is the idea that their weakness has decreased their personal value. When I was a young man in the late 1970s, I worked for a time in a large nursing home that was located in Northern California. I had always loved older people and I enjoyed caring for the old men in my unit; most of whom had come over from Italy in the early 1900s to work in the lumber industry. Anyone who has ever worked in one of these places will tell you that most older people, when first admitted, will usually still have most of their faculties. But in a very short time they tend to join the ranks of the vacant-eyed residents in wheelchairs who line the halls of every nursing home. I discovered in my time of working there that this transformation didn't happen purely for physical reasons, but when they started to lose their sense of value. The few who avoided that fate were always those who discovered a useful role on the ward. One of my favorites was a rough old man who was confined to a wheelchair. He would fill his days making beautiful macramé hanging baskets that were filled with plants throughout the nursing home. I doubt that this tough old logger had ever seen a macramé basket back in his younger days but having a new purpose for a new season enabled him to retain his own sense of value. People lined up to buy his hanging baskets!

If we are ever going to really understand the historic Jesus, we must deeply understand the nature of his relationship with the Father. It wasn't something that was peripheral to his ministry, the Father was right at the center of everything he did! Out of that relationship came his motivation to do ministry upon the earth. Out of that relationship came all of the resources that he used to preach and heal and proclaim the kingdom of God. Out of that relationship came his identity as the Son of the living God. This is the great example that Jesus came to demonstrate for us, and this is the way we must follow if we are to resemble Jesus. Not just by looking at his teaching but looking at the central nature of his relationship with the Father!

Questions to Consider

1. If the key to understanding Jesus is found in the centrality of his relationship with the Father, how does this change your understanding of yourself as a Jesus-follower?

2. The first major area in the life of Christ that flowed out of his relationship with the Father was his motivation for ministry: He came because he had been sent. What motivates you in your career or ministry? Do you agree that a sense of responsibility can never be our primary motive for doing things? Explain why.

3. The second major area in the life of Christ that flowed out of his relationship with the Father were his resources for ministry. His vision and abilities and endurance were all dependent on his relationship with the Father. Where do the resources come from that you use in your ministry or career? How dependent are they on your relationship with God?

4. The third major area in the life of Christ that flowed out of his relationship with the Father was his identity as a person. He deliberately chose to only see himself as a son. What is your identity based on? Why is it important to find the right measurement when determining your true value?

One Transition Leads to Another

I didn't grow up with much interest in God or his church, so when I finally met him, I had to initially make the transition from stranger to Lord. My earliest memory as a newly saved Christian was not one of blessings but of deep brokenness. In the days that followed my salvation, when people would ask, "how are you doing Ralph?" I would break down in tears as I attempted to reply. It was a bit embarrassing. Yet, for me, it was a very necessary transition from being in control of my life to relinquishing that control forever. I had to learn a lot in those first months about what pleased the Lord and what did not.

In the years to come, as I continued down the path that he was preparing for me, I discovered that this first transition was now leading me to a second – from Lord to Father. As I've tried to illustrate in this book, it was a transition that involved many moving parts: False portraits of "father" had to be scrubbed clean in order for the Holy Spirit to paint a more realistic likeness in my mind. Using scripture as his medium, he began a process of revealing his love, provision, correction and even his jealous heart over me. This transition was absolutely essential, for much of what God wanted to do in my life had to be done by a Father, not just a Lord.

As I started to explore this intimate relationship with God as my Father, I found that there are actually different stages of sonship: There is a time when a son enjoys and grows in his childhood, but there is also a stage when a son must put away childish things and become a full-grown man! (See I Corinthians 13:11). C.S. Lewis said, "Mere improvement is not redemption, though redemption always improves people. God became man to turn creatures into sons: not simply to produce better men of the old kind but to produce a new kind of man." (CS Lewis / Mere Christianity). I began to realize that there was, in fact, still another transition that I would have to embrace in order to continue in my Christian growth – from son to man.

A New Kind of Person

Whatever view we might hold about the theory of evolution; we can mostly agree that there is a natural process of selection where one creature develops into a stronger or more efficient type of creature in order to survive. A classic example can be found in the history of the area around London, England in the mid-eighteenth century. When it still had a mostly farming economy, the most prevalent type of moths to be found around the city was a species called the White Peppered Moth (Biston Betularia). It's light coloring helped it blend in with the lichen-covered trees and whitewashed buildings throughout the city. However, as the industrial revolution began in London, the soot from coal burning factories began to darken the trees and the buildings. The result was that the White Peppered Moth became an easy target for birds, and the much rarer Black Peppered Moth now blended in and eventually became the dominant species. Because we see this evidence of natural selection in the world around us, it's logical to think that, at the dawn of time, human beings would have had to also evolve into creatures who were bigger and stronger than the fierce animals living around them. Instead, God took the evolutionary process in a completely new direction. He gave the earth a creature made in his image, one who would conquer through intellect and invention, not bigger muscles and teeth. In fact, God's very first command to the first man and woman was to be fruitful and rule over every creature that moves on the ground (See Genesis 1:28). For better or worse, humans (made in the image of God) took the planet down a very different evolutionary path than before the appearance of Adam and Eve.

I love science fiction books and movies. I especially love the ones that go far ahead in time and give a glimpse of what mankind might be like in the distant future. One of my early memories is watching, with my mom, the old classic movie based on H.G. Wells novel "The Time Machine." I found it fascinating to see cities rise and fall around the professor as he sat in his old-fashioned-looking machine, racing through eons of time. At the end of the journey, he discovers that one fiercer and more intelligent type of man has evolved into a place of dominance over the others (who now are a food source like cattle). This story reflects our tendency to think that evolution will always lead to greater and greater human intellect and invention as natural selection does its work. But could it be possible that God, once more, has a completely different evolutionary direction for human beings? There are several tantalizing glimpses of this to be found in the Bible. In the book of Ephesians, we are told to, "put off, concerning your former conduct, the old man and put on the new man which was created according to God, in true righteousness and holiness" (Ephesians 4:22-24). Notice here that Paul didn't say they were to improve their old conduct and become better men – he told them to put on a new kind of man! Apparently, the early Christians understood that the goal of Christianity was not a *moral goal* of trying to be better men and women, but an *evolutionary goal* of becoming a new species of men and women. To quote C.S. Lewis again: "Now, if you care to talk in these terms, the Christian view is precisely that the Next Step has already appeared. And it is really new. It is not a change from brainy men to brainier men: it is a change that goes off in a totally different direction—a change from being creatures of God to being sons of God. The first instance appearing in Palestine two thousand years ago" (C.S. Lewis / Mere Christianity). This is such a radical way of understanding the work of Jesus. He did indeed come to pay the penalty for our sins, but once that penalty had been paid, there was now available (to anyone who would come to the cross) a pathway to be transformed into a completely new kind of person!

It's very tempting for Christians to think that Jesus the man was a unique kind of person who would never walk the earth again – but the truth is that he was the first fruit of many persons who will one day fill the earth! The bible says it this way: "So it is written: The first man Adam became a living being"; the last Adam, a life-giving spirit. And just as we have borne the image of the earthly man, so shall we bear the image of the heavenly man" (1 Corinthians 15:45, 49). If this passage were only referring to what will one day happen in heaven, it would have made no sense for Paul to have exhorted his Ephesian disciples to, "put on the new man which was created according to God, in true righteousness and holiness" (Ephesians 4:24). The first Christians really seemed to believe that sons and daughters of the Father were now meant to *pursue a new transition* in their Christian growth: from people who bear the image of the earthly man, to those who bear the image of the heavenly man. To quote C. S. Lewis again: "We were previously considering the Christian idea of 'putting on Christ.' What I want to make clear is that this is not one among many jobs a Christian has to do; and it is not a sort of special exercise for the top class. It is the whole of Christianity. Christianity offers nothing else at all" (C.S. Lewis / Mere Christianity). To embrace this truth is to have one's whole understanding of the purpose of Christianity upended! The early Christians understood that the goal of their salvation was not to become nicer people or even to go to heaven in the end – It was to become little Christs! To become images of the Heavenly Man who would draw others into his transforming and life-giving embrace. When we pray "Our Father in heaven... your kingdom come" it must be with the understanding that his kingdom comes not through political or even religious upheaval, but through the process of individual people becoming new creations. Let's look closer at how this process works in our lives.

A New Kind of Process

It's worth repeating that this process of becoming a new kind of person is not a process of self-improvement or even good works; it's not something that will only happen after we die (that will be its culmination, not its beginning). So, what exactly is this process of transformation from son or daughter to a new kind of man or woman? Let's try to answer that question in four ways:

1. The Father will be satisfied with nothing less.

Before we look at the process itself, we must firmly grasp how important this is to God. In our walk with him, it's normal (and correct) to bring to him our requests and to look for his encouragement. Every good Father wants to be involved in the details of his children's lives. But every father also wants the very best for his children, and with our Heavenly Father, that desire is magnified to the ultimate degree. Like fathers everywhere, he is immensely pleased the first time that we stand and take an unsteady step – but he won't be finished with us until we are walking freely on the path that he has chosen. Jesus expressed this desire in a way that has been misunderstood from almost the moment he uttered it: "Be perfect, therefore, as your heavenly Father is perfect" (Matthew 5:48). Throughout the history of the church, well-meaning Christians have interpreted those words in two ways: either as a command to achieve some kind of sinless perfection, or a promise of what we will achieve one day in heaven. But there is a third way to understand this statement. The word "perfect" in the Greek is the word, *"Teleios."* When it's used to describe God it means, "Wanting nothing necessary to completeness" but when it's used to describe man it means, "full grown, adult, of full age, mature" (See

Strong's G5046). With this understanding, we start to realize that Jesus wasn't commanding us to live a life free from mistakes – he was telling us to live like adults! The Message Bible says it this way: "In a word, what I'm saying is, Grow up. You're kingdom subjects. Now live like it. Live out your God-created identity" (Matthew 5:48 MSG).

Unfortunately, we often have a tendency to see the Father in the same way as the family dentist we had as children. I inherited rather bad teeth from my parents. That (along with my bad brushing habits) meant that I had frequent toothaches. I wanted relief from the pain, but I knew that if I went to the dentist it would lead to a whole series of procedures as he uncovered cavity after cavity. I wanted the immediate relief that he would bring, but I didn't particularly want the process that would lead to healthy teeth. In the same way, we are quick to come to God in a crisis, but once he has answered those prayers, we feel fairly satisfied with things the way they are – unfortunately, he is not! C. S. Lewis said it this way: "On the one hand, God's demand for perfection need not discourage you in the least in your present attempts to be good, or even in your present failures. On the other hand, you must realize from the outset that the goal towards which He is beginning to guide you is absolute perfection; and no power in the whole universe, except you yourself, can prevent Him from taking you to that goal. That is what you are in for" (C.S. Lewis/Mere Christianity).

2. The process starts when we put our full attention upon Jesus.

It's hard to let go of the idea that the process of becoming a new kind of man must start with improving the old kind of man. But we can never really begin the process if we try to start there. Self-improvement is just the opposite of what is needed. The Apostle Paul said it this way in II Corinthians 3:18. "And we all, who with unveiled faces contemplate the Lord's glory, are being transformed into his image with ever-increasing glory, which comes from the Lord, who is the Spirit." There is a promise in this verse that sounds almost too good to be true – that we will be transformed into the image of Jesus! Many believers assume that this is something that happens automatically as we go to church and seek to live out a "normal" Christian life. However, just as we must choose to make the transition from Lord to Father, we must also choose to make the transition from child to adult. Let's take a closer look at how it starts in the life of a believer. Paul said, "We all, who with unveiled faces contemplate the Lord's glory" (II Corinthians 3:18). Notice that there is a two-part action being described in this sentence: To "unveil" our face and then to "contemplate" his glory. This is something more than having positive thoughts about Jesus, so let's look at what these words actually mean.

The word "unveiled" in the Greek is the word: *"anakalypto"* which means to open or uncover something (See Strong's G343). It's interesting that Paul didn't say we should start by just contemplating Jesus, but that this contemplation should be done in a very unique way – with an unveiled face. The imagery being used here suggests that transformation depends on our willingness to pull back the veil; to fully expose ourselves to the presence of God. Embracing a vulnerability and intimacy similar to that of a woman in Bible times who unveils her face to her husband or her closest friends. Honestly, I find it much easier to keep the veil on in my quiet times with God. I am a very structured kind of person, so it's easy to incorporate contemplating into a daily schedule without revealing too much in the process. I've begun to realize, however, that personal discipline can only take one so far in this third kind of transition. Apparently, you must have an uncovered face before you can look deeply into his!

The second word in this two-step process is "contemplate." In the Greek it's the word: *"katoptrizo"* and it presented some challenges to the early bible translators. The literal meaning of this word is: "To show in a mirror, to make to reflect, to mirror" (See Strong's G2734). This is why early scholars translated it to read, "But we all, with open face beholding as in a glass the glory of the Lord" (KJV). Later translations simplified it to say, "beholding the Lord's glory" (ESV). But have we missed something important that is being said in the Greek? It helps to think about how we "contemplate" the reflection in our own bathroom mirror each morning. We look at the details of that face as we get ready for the day. We think about what that reflection is telling us about ourselves ("I am looking old" or "I look fit today"). We use that reflection to help us make improvements to the face that we are beholding; whether it's brushing our hair or rearranging our makeup. The point is this: whatever we are doing as we look into that glass; we are giving it our full and undivided attention. It's important to realize that we are to contemplate the words and the character and the glory of Jesus in exactly the same way! In these days of multi-tasking, there is very little that commands our full attention. Perhaps this is the reason why modern Christians don't appear much different than anyone else in our society. What was supposed to make us different was never just what we believe, but who we resemble, and that change in likeness only comes when we learn to deeply contemplate his glory.

Recently I've begun to experiment with silence. When you read the writings of the early church fathers, you get the impression that silence was a much bigger part of their training than it is today. In the 1600s silence became so popular that it grew into a full-blown religious revival known as "Quietism." It's founder, Miguel de Molinos, once said, "In the throne of silence are manifest the perfections of spiritual beauty." Throughout the early centuries in church history there were many times when men and women would isolate themselves into communities that emphasized silence and contemplation. After deciding to try it for myself, I was humbled by the fact that – silence is tough! I found it difficult to even quiet my mind for the time it took to count down two minutes! Perhaps this difficulty that we have in silencing our inner voice has a much greater consequence than just having over-busy lives. Could it be the main barrier that keeps us from contemplating with an unveiled face, and making the transition from a person to a new kind of person? Notice also that the object of our unveiled attention was never meant to be our prayer list but "to contemplate the Lord's glory" (II Corinthians 3:18). The word "glory" is an interesting one in the Greek. It is the word: *"doxa"* and it's meaning is, "The absolutely perfect inward or personal excellency of Christ; the majesty" (See Strong's G1391). This verse is not describing an experience of *feeling* his glory as we gaze upon Christ, it is describing the act of *looking* into his glory. So often I find in my own quiet times that I might be contemplating the story of Christ (or even the words of Christ) but I'm not looking at Christ himself! I'm not paying attention to what all of these elements say about the glory of Christ. But could it be that this is the one action that will change me more than any bible study or church service ever could? So, this process of transforming into "little Jesus" images only starts when we learn to contemplate, with unveiled faces, the glory of Jesus. But once it has started, how do we stay on track? How can we know, over the years, if we are still heading towards the right goal? Let's look at one sure way to know.

3. The continuation of this process requires a daily renewing of the mind

When it comes to the way I think about things, I have to confess that there have been many changes over the years. These were not revisions that I consciously made to my thoughts, but changes that were *molded* through circumstances and life experience. Growing up in the 1960s in segregated Alabama, my thoughts towards people of color were as racist as the tiki-torch-carrying Proud Boys we saw on television. Attending college changed that thinking and later, living among the people of many cultures changed it even more. Even as a Christian, my thinking went through many alterations: from a prosperity gospel to a political gospel to an information-based gospel to a Jesus-centered gospel. I share this because, whether we realize it or not, the way that we think is constantly mutating and evolving. A change in thinking can be a good thing, but it's important to realize that a renewal in thinking is something very different. To understand the difference, let's look at what the apostle Paul had to say about renewal: "Do not conform to the pattern of this world but be transformed by the renewing of your mind. Then you will be able to test and approve what God's will is—his good, pleasing and perfect will" (Romans 12:2). Notice here that Paul draws a distinction between thoughts that are changed by conforming and thoughts that are changed by renewing. For much of my life, my thinking was changed by simply conforming to the life-situations that I was immersed in. Everyone I knew in my segregated high school was racist, so I thought like a racist. Later, everyone I knew in college and in the hippie-counterculture were political liberals, so I thought like a liberal. I was saved in a Pentecostal denomination, so my thoughts about the gospel conformed to much of what I heard being preached in my church. They were all patterns that my mind conformed to. But Paul points out that conforming the mind, even to good patterns, does not equal transformation

-- only a renewing of the mind transforms. The word translated "renewing" in the Greek is the word: *"anakainosis"* and it means: "a renewal, a renovation, a complete change for the better" (See Strong's G342). When you renew or renovate something, you are not rearranging the furniture, you are tearing it down and starting over!

So, the question arises: what does a renewed mind actually look like? We see that it is something more than just conforming to the latest teaching, so what is this new mind? It helps to remember that this transition is not from the old man to a better man, it is a transition from the old man to the image of Christ. To quote the Apostle Paul in II Corinthians 2:16. "Who has known the mind of the Lord so as to instruct him? But we have the mind of Christ." I don't believe that Paul was being poetic when he said that he had the mind of Christ. I am certain that he (and most other first century Christians) truly believed that, because Christ lived in them,

they had *access* to the mind of Christ! In the early days of organizing the church, Barnabas and Saul weren't elected to be missionary church planters, God chose them while they were participating in a worship service. (See Acts 13:2). Later in his ministry, when Paul and his companions were on the road, the Holy Spirit turned them from their plan to preach in the province of Asia and instead, directed them to the region of Galatia (See Acts 16:6). These are just two examples of many instances where believers accessed the mind of Christ. These stories in the Bible sound very dramatic and we tend to think to ourselves, "I could never be that advanced" but the truth is that anyone who has said, "Christ come into my heart" has free access to the one who lives there! So, in those times when I am trying to evaluate whether I'm still on track, it does little good to look at my good works or my religious activities. The safest way to verify the path that I am on is to simply ask myself: "Is my way of thinking conforming to the patterns around me, or am I daily accessing the mind of Christ?

4. The measurement of this process is love

It is, of course, important to know if I'm on track in this new evolutionary pathway that God has created for mankind, but what about the journey itself? It is certainly possible to be on the right road but walking so slowly that it will take forever to get there! How can I measure my progress? Because this transition is not from the old man to a better man, many of the ways that we would normally measure progress can be deceiving. Things can look good at the moment but slowly change as we continue down the path. Churches can grow big and then reverse direction over the years. Personal spiritual gifts can work powerfully for a while, but then diminish as we get older. Even personal integrity can have its ups and downs. So, if this transition cannot be measured by temporal things, is there something eternal that can accurately mark our progress? The Bible clearly points to three things that are eternal, and then proceeds to show us which of those three is the greatest. In I Corinthians 13:13 it says, "And now these three remain: faith, hope and love. But the greatest of these is love." Faith and hope are good indicators of how we are doing, but by far the greatest way to measure this transition is the measuring line of love! Why is love the greatest? Was it just an arbitrary designation made by God, or are there strong and logical reasons to name love as the most important? Let's close this chapter by looking at some of those reasons.

Love measures the level of our development as disciples

"A new commandment I give to you, that you love one another: just as I have loved you, you also are to love one another. By this all people will know that you are my disciples, if you have love for one another" (John 13:35). Notice that Jesus didn't say, "this is one of the ways that they will know you are my followers." He said, "by *this* (and apparently only by this) will all people recognize that you are my disciples." It's a little shocking to realize that what marks me as a disciple of Jesus in the eyes of the world is not the church I belong to, but the amount of love that is evident in my life! Could it be that the reason why so many disciples are invisible in the world today is not for a lack of boldness, but for a lack of love? It's so easy to only measure our progress as believers according to our spiritual maturity while completely ignoring our emotional maturity. Peter Scazzero in his ground-breaking book Emotional Healthy Spirituality said it this way: "Emotional health and spiritual maturity are inseparable. It is not possible to be spiritually mature while remaining emotionally immature... loving well is the goal of the Christian life"

(Peter Scazzero/Emotionally Healthy Spirituality). If loving well really is the goal, then only love can reveal how much we have developed towards that goal.

Love measures the worth of our gifts and talents

"If I have prophetic powers, and understand all mysteries and all knowledge, and if I have all faith, so as to remove mountains, but have not love, I am nothing" (I Corinthians 13: 1-2). In the forty-plus years that I have followed Jesus, I've been exposed to a lot of different ministries that highlighted different spiritual gifts. In my early years in Alabama, I attended revival services under big top tents with sawdust on the floor. In one of those meetings, I saw an entire thirty-member choir fall down under the power of the Holy Spirit. I have been in countless healing services and prophetic conferences and I have witnessed great acts of faith on the mission field. What I didn't realize in those years was that the *value* of all those gifts was never meant to be measured by how powerful or successful they seemed. According to Paul, even the person who has gifts that can move mountains is nothing (has no value) without love! I have come to realize that, when evaluating the real value of the ministry God has called me to, the only accurate measurement is: (1) was it motivated by love? and (2) did it produce greater love in the recipients of my ministry? It's frightening to realize just how easily we can be deceived into thinking that a great ministry gift equals great progress in the kingdom!

Love measures how in-focus we are as images of Christ

I John 4:12 "No one has ever seen God; if we love one another, God abides in us and his love is perfected in us." There is an important concept in this small verse that can easily be overlooked when reading through our bible every morning. It starts with an unequivocal statement: "No one has ever seen God." Many Christians tend to stop there, believing that God is invisible and pretty much unknowable. However, the next statement is radical. "if we love one another, God abides in us." It is true that when we are saved, God starts to reveal himself in our lives, but when we choose to practice this greatest eternal element – he abides in us and people start to see him in us! Back in my Jesus Freak days, I thought that it was my long hair and my radical lifestyle that kept me in focus as a Jesus follower. Now I know, without a shadow of a doubt, that it is my love. Every time that I am kind to another person, treating him as a unique and special creation, I am bringing into sharper focus the image of Jesus upon my life. We must never forget that the ultimate endgame of Christianity is not just to tell people about Jesus – it is to be transformed into Jesus – and nothing brings him into clearer focus than our choice to love one another!

Because the Father loves us in the way that all good fathers love their children, he will not be satisfied with a cute little toddler, holding his hand. He will relentlessly begin to steer us towards the real goal of the Christian journey: not just going to heaven but growing into a new kind of person.

It is a process that he demands of us and it is one that requires we put our full attention on Jesus, seeking him first, before all other thing in our lives. It is a process that works not through conforming to religious patterns but transforming through a renewal of our minds. Our progress in this process can be as accurately measured as any scientific apparatus can measure. We only have to look at our love for one another.

Questions to Consider

1.   If the goal of Christianity is not a moral goal of trying to be better men and women, but an evolutionary goal of becoming a new species of men and women – how does that change your understanding of following Jesus?

2.   If transformation comes, not from good works, but from contemplating his glory with an unveiled face; what needs to change in your daily walk with Jesus?

3.   What is the difference between a mind that is conformed to the patterns of this world (including the religious world) and a mind that is transformed by the renewing of the Holy Spirit?

4.   Since it is possible to be on the right road but still not be making much progress, explain why love is the best measure of your progress.

Afterword

As we come to the end of this book about changing the nature of our relationship with God, it might be instructive to repeat the words of my favorite writer, C.S. Lewis: "Mere improvement is not redemption, though redemption always improves people. God became man to turn creatures into sons" (CS Lewis / Mere Christianity). As Christians, we all know that Jesus came to redeem our lives through his sacrifice upon the cross – but redemption for what purpose? That is the great question that we must answer if we intend to go into all the world and preach the gospel. The good news is not that God will improve the human creatures he has made – it is that he has chosen to turn those creatures into sons and daughters! That is the purpose of the redemption that we have in Jesus.

Making the transition in our relationship with God from Lord to Father must never be seen as a way of improving our situation or increasing our comfort-level as followers of Jesus. For most of us, just the opposite will be true. Changing the nature of our relationship with God will inevitably change our relationship with the world as well. As we step away from the world's definitions and embrace our identity as sons and daughters, we will find ourselves in the rather uncomfortable position of being a light shining on a hill, not hidden under a basket. As we grow in our intimacy with the Father, we will also grow more aware that he wants all of who we are and that he intends to transform who we are into a true image of his Son.

Change is never easy. It forces us to release things in our lives that we've become comfortable with and to step into places where we cannot trust in ourselves. The truth about this Christian experience is really a very simple one: a person will only have as much of God as he or she really wants. It is my prayer that we will always want more!